FACES OF DISCOVERY: CHILDREN WHO ASKED QUESTIONS!

BY CAROLYN COLE REYNARD
AND TERESA E BRUSCO

First published by Ultimate World Publishing 2024

ISBN

Paperback: 978-1-923255-44-9
Ebook: 978-1-923255-45-6

Cover design: Ultimate World Publishing
Layout and typesetting: Ultimate World Publishing
Editor: Marnae Kelley

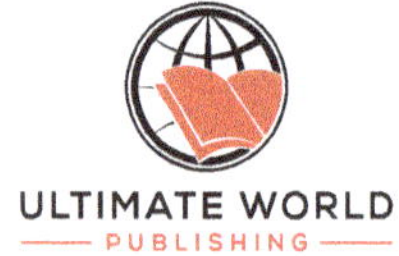

Ultimate World Publishing
Diamond Creek,
Victoria Australia 3089
www.writeabook.com.au

CONTENTS

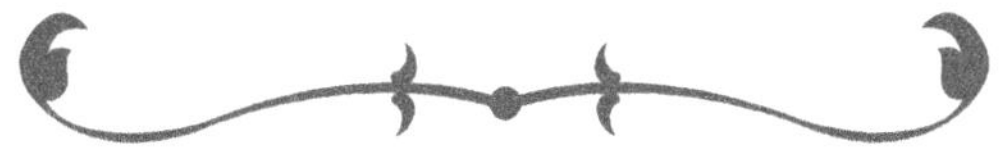

DEDICATION TO YOU, THE READER, AND YOUR CAREGIVERS

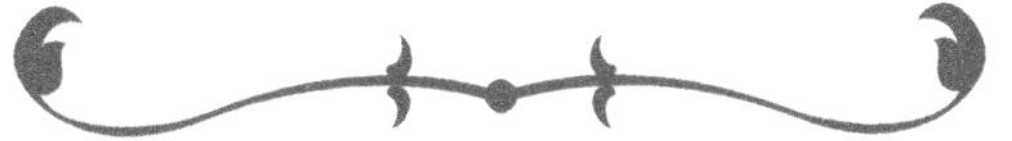

This special book has been created by the author and illustrator just for you. We wrote these passages and painted these portraits to encourage you to think and ask questions about everything you see around you. It's also a way to show how scientists long ago worked together to discover new things. We want you to remember that when we work together, we can achieve amazing things.

At the end of each part of the book, you'll find questions designed just for you, the reader. These questions are meant to help you think about how the lives and discoveries of these scientists connect to your own life. We hope these questions will spark your curiosity and help you see how remarkable these scientists were.

Caregivers, thank you for joining your child on this adventure through the pages of this book. Your support and encouragement are invaluable as they explore and learn about the world around them.

Are you ready to join us on a journey of exploration and wonder? Let's begin!

With excitement and curiosity,

The artist and the author

INTRODUCTION

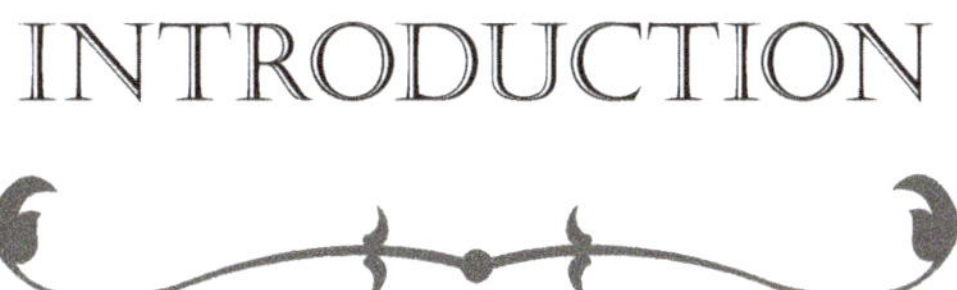

Welcome to *Faces of Discovery*, where you'll find portraits painted by Carolyn Reynard, each visually telling the story of a scientist's life and achievements. Carolyn Reynard carefully researched the fascinating histories of these scientists, uncovering their remarkable discoveries, which she captured in each portrait. Take a close look at each painting to discover hints of these extraordinary moments!

Next to each portrait, you'll discover a passage that introduces the scientist in a fun and easy to understand way, even for the youngest explorers! This consistent format will guide you through their lives and the work that made them famous. If you want to learn more about specific scientific theories, laws, and experiments mentioned, you can explore further with the help of a grown-up or on your own.

The chapters in this book are organized by different fields of science, arranged in a specific order to illustrate how each scientist's observations or discoveries supported later scientists in that same field.

Just as each scientist learned from those who came before them, Mrs. Reynard and Mrs. Brusco used recent scientific discoveries or applications such as AI, the internet, and other digital techniques to create this project. By combining these new discoveries with their imagination and creativity, they've brought this book to life!

Get ready to embark on a journey through the lives of these extraordinary scientists, told through art and stories!

CHAPTER 1

EXPLORERS OF THE WORLD WE SEE

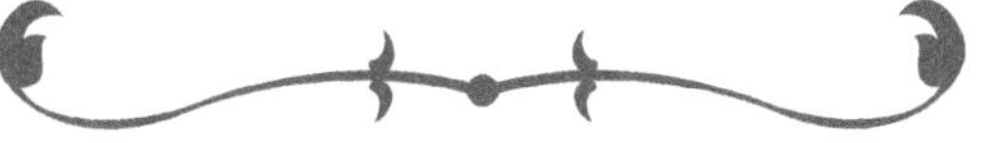

ARISTOTLE: UNRAVELING NATURE'S MYSTERIES
384 BCE–322 BCE

Long ago, there was a really smart man named Aristotle. He was born more than 2,000 years ago in Greece. Even when Aristotle was a little boy, he loved asking questions about everything around him. He was super curious!

As a child, Aristotle liked to explore nature. He would spend time outside, watching animals and plants closely. He noticed how they moved, what they ate, and how they lived. This made him want to learn even more about the world.

When he grew up, Aristotle became a scientist and a teacher. He studied many things, like animals, plants, and even the stars in the sky. He wrote lots of books about what he discovered. One of the coolest things Aristotle did was classify animals into groups based on how they looked and acted. This helped people understand animals better.

Aristotle also thought about big questions, like how the Earth worked and why things happened. He came up with ideas that people still learn about today. For example, he figured out that the Earth was round, not flat!

Aristotle didn't just study nature; he also taught many students who became famous scientists themselves. He loved sharing what he knew with others.

Even though Aristotle lived a long time ago, his ideas and discoveries changed how people think about the world. He showed us that being curious and asking questions can help us learn amazing things about nature and how everything fits together.

So, the next time you see a bird flying or a flower growing, think of Aristotle and how he wanted to understand everything around him! What's something you're curious about and would like to learn more, just like Aristotle?

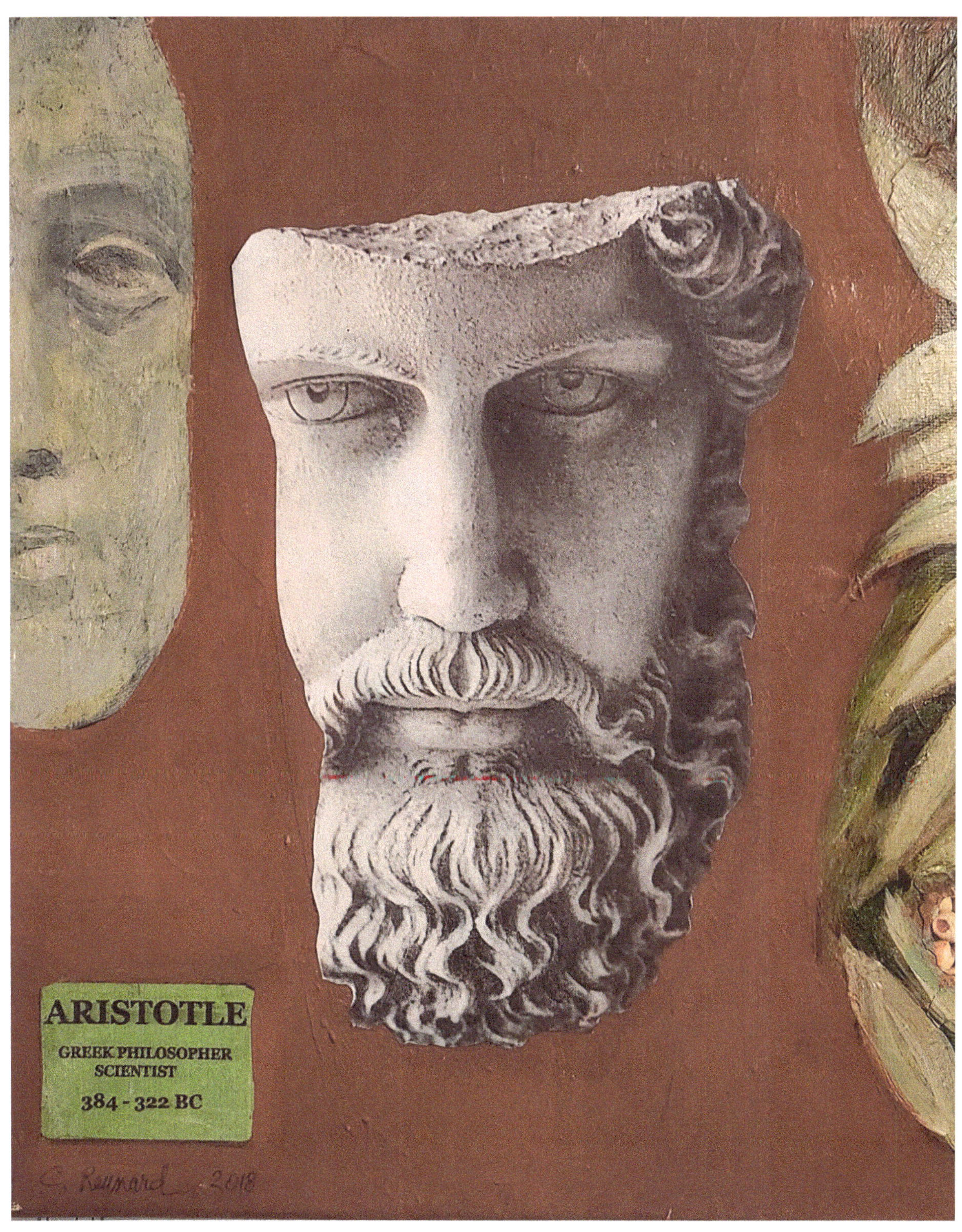
ARISTOTLE
GREEK PHILOSOPHER
SCIENTIST
384 - 322 BC

CHARLES DARWIN:
JOURNEY OF EVOLUTIONARY DISCOVERY
1809–1882

Charles Darwin was a curious and adventurous man who loved exploring nature. Imagine someone who loves going on adventures to faraway places, looking at all kinds of plants and animals, and asking lots of questions about them. That was Darwin!

When he was young, Darwin went on a long journey around the world on a ship called the HMS Beagle. He visited many different places and saw amazing animals and plants that he had never seen before. He collected lots of specimens and took careful notes about everything he saw.

Darwin noticed something very interesting: different animals of the same kind had special features that helped them survive in their particular environments. For example, he saw that birds called finches on different islands had different beak shapes, depending on what they ate.

From his study of other scientists' observations, including Aristotle's, Darwin came up with a big idea called evolution. He realized that over a long time, plants and animals change to adapt to their environments. This process is called natural selection, where the animals and plants that are best suited to their environment survive and have babies, passing on their special features.

Darwin's ideas helped us understand how all living things are connected and how they have changed over millions of years. He wrote a famous book called *On the Origin of Species* to share his discoveries with the world.

So, Charles Darwin was like a nature detective who figured out the secret of how animals and plants change over time. His discoveries helped us understand the amazing variety of life on Earth! Have you ever observed animals or plants in your environment and noticed how they adapt to survive?

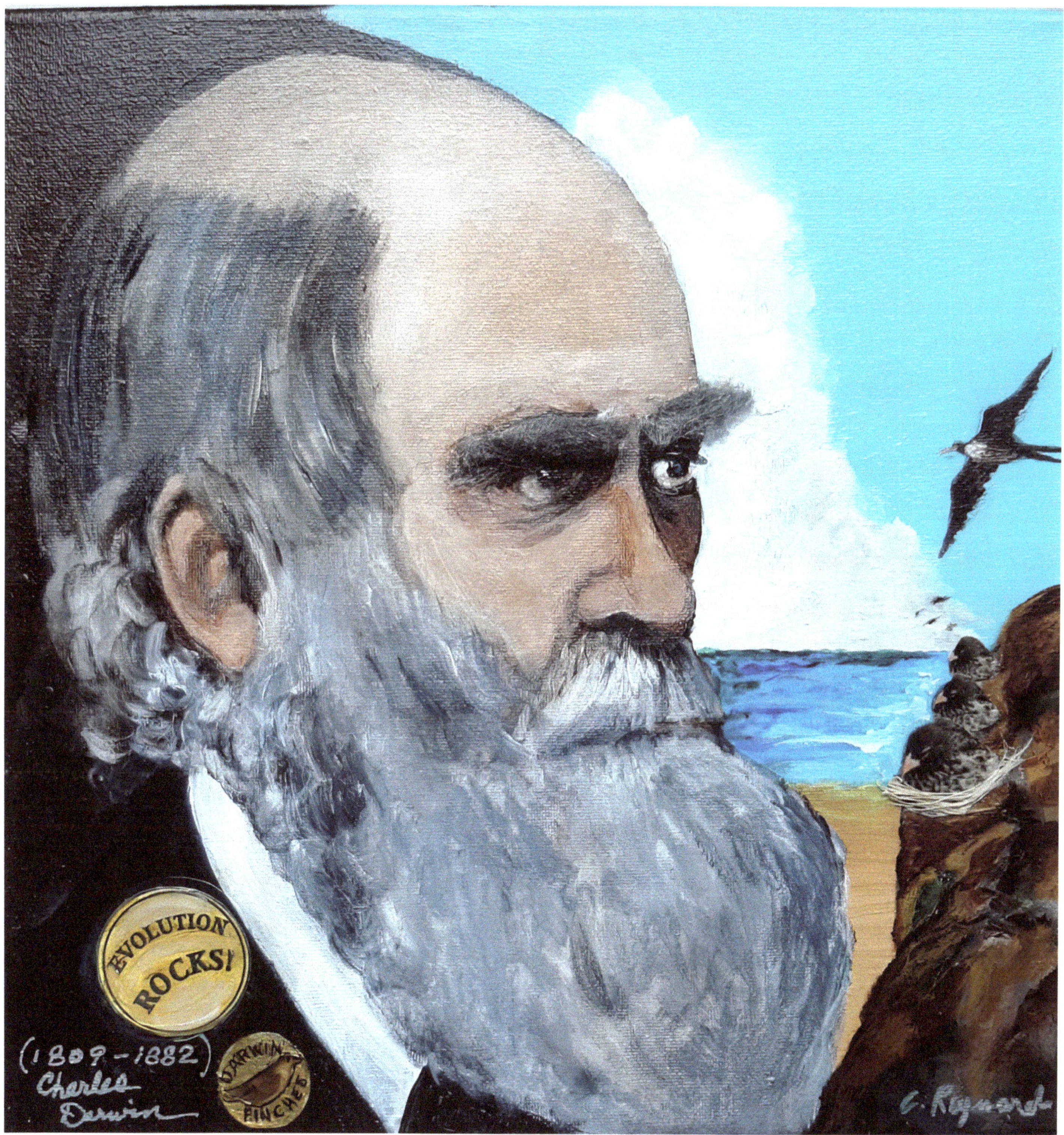

EVOLUTION ROCKS!
DARWIN FINCHES
(1809 - 1882)
Charles Darwin
C. Regnard

ERNST HAECKEL:
CHARTING THE DEPTHS OF NATURE'S BEAUTY
1834–1919

Ernst Haeckel was a scientist who lived in Germany in the 1800s and early 1900s. He was interested in studying animals and plants in the ocean, which is called marine biology. As a child, Ernst loved exploring nature and learning about different creatures.

One of his big ideas was that all living things are related to each other and have changed over time. This idea was inspired by Charles Darwin, who said animals and plants evolve, or change slowly over many years to fit better in their environments. Haeckel used Darwin's ideas to study how creatures in the ocean evolved and how they are all connected.

Haeckel also drew detailed pictures of tiny sea creatures called microorganisms. His drawings helped scientists understand these creatures better.

Even though Haeckel didn't discover a specific thing like a new animal or plant, his ideas about evolution and his drawings were really important. They helped people understand how life on Earth has changed over millions of years, and they still teach us a lot about the natural world today!

Ernst Haeckel explored the diversity of life through his drawings and studies. What's a creature or plant you find fascinating to study and draw, like Haeckel?

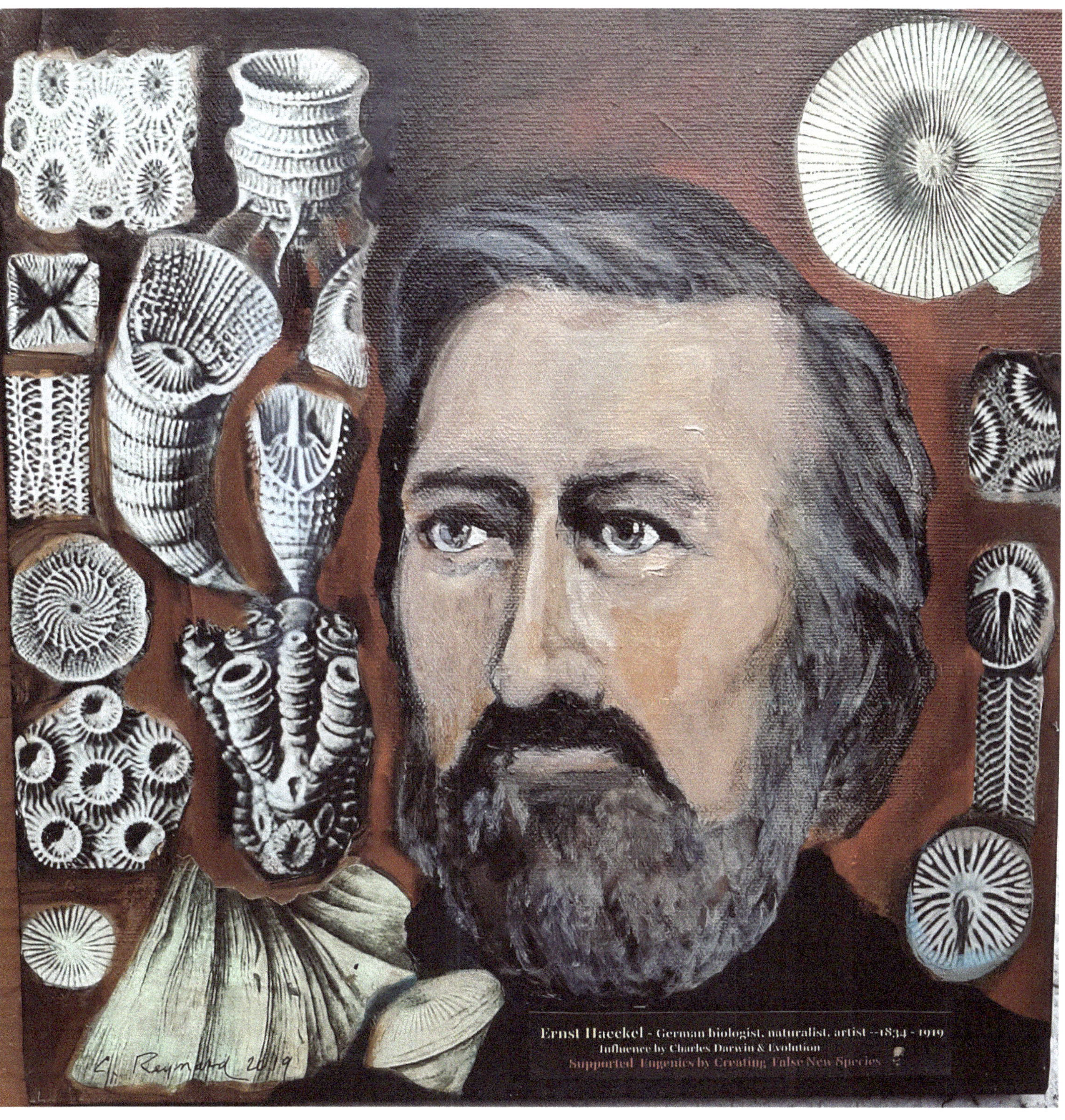
Reynard 2019
Ernst Haeckel - German biologist, naturalist, artist - 1834 - 1919
Influence by Charles Darwin & Evolution
Supported Eugenics by Creating False New Species

CHAPTER 2

TRAILBLAZERS OF EARTH'S STORY

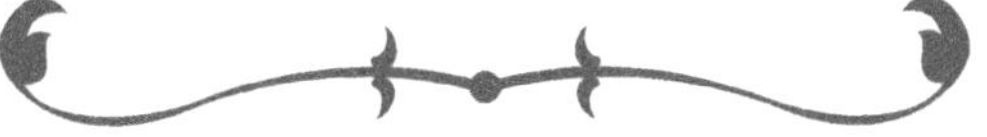

Georgius Agricola:
Unearthing Secrets
1494–1555

A long time ago, there was a scientist named Georgius Agricola. He lived in the 1500s in Germany. Georgius, who was also called Georg, was a curious boy who loved exploring the world around him. He was especially fascinated by rocks and minerals.

As a child, Georg liked to go on adventures in the mountains near his home. He would climb rocks and collect shiny stones that caught his eye. His parents noticed how much he loved rocks and encouraged him to learn more about them.

When Georg grew up, he became a mineralogist and a metallurgist. That means he studied rocks and minerals and how metals are made. He wanted to understand where metals like gold and silver came from and how they could be turned into useful things.

One of Georg's biggest discoveries was about how miners could find valuable metals in the ground. He wrote a famous book called *De Re Metallica*, which in English, means *"On the Nature of Metals."* In this book, Georg described how to dig mines safely and how to process metals like copper and iron.

Georg Agricola also studied how minerals form in the earth and how they can be used in medicine and industry. He wrote many books and drew detailed pictures of rocks and mining techniques to teach others about what he learned.

Even though Georg lived a long time ago, his ideas are still used in geology and mining today. Scientists and miners still read his books to understand how to find and use metals. Georg Agricola showed us that by exploring and studying rocks and minerals, we can make amazing discoveries about the Earth and how it works!

What's something you've found in nature that you think might be interesting to learn more about?

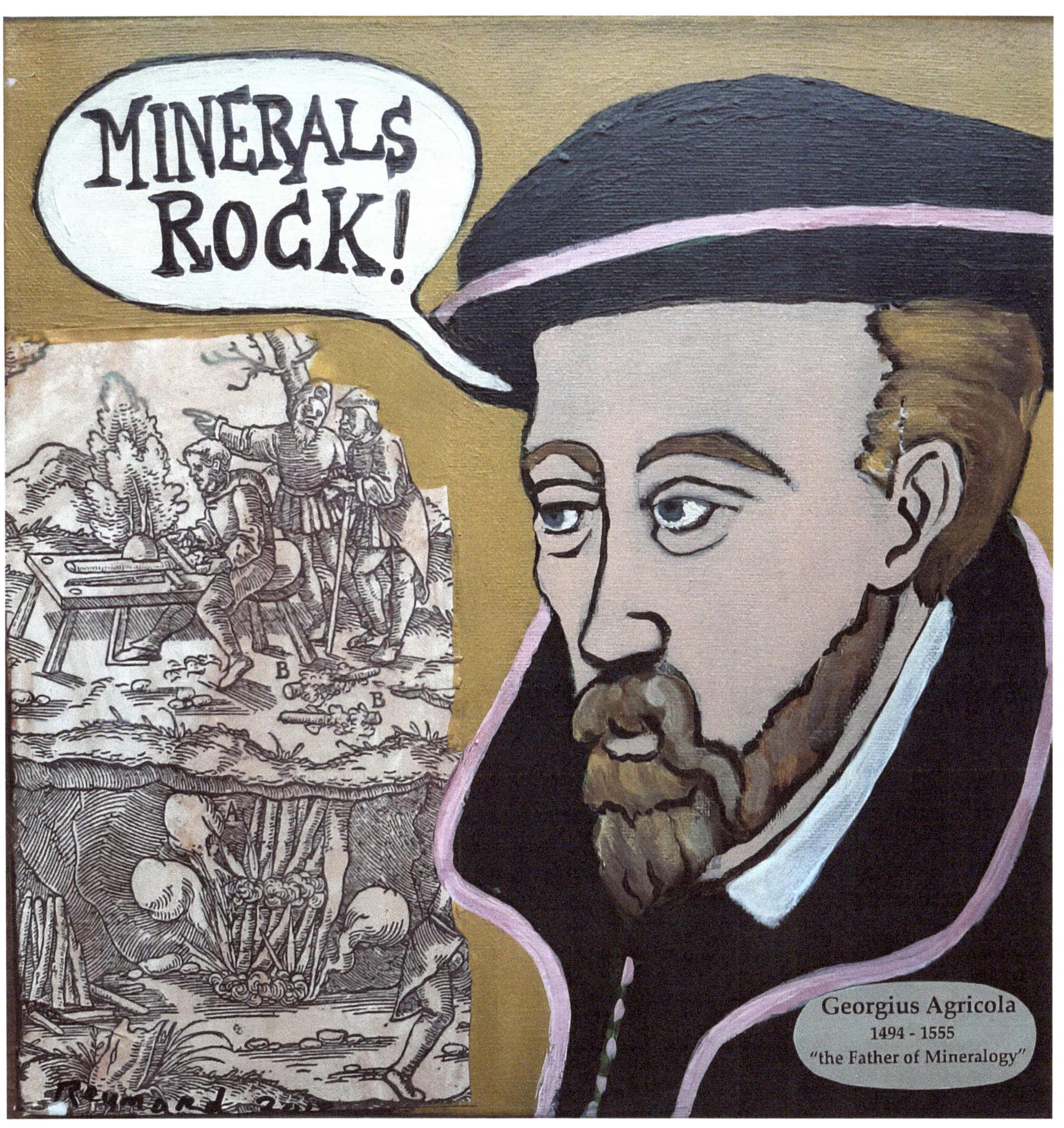

MINERALS ROCK!
Georgius Agricola
1494 - 1555
"the Father of Mineralogy"

JAMES HUTTON:
DISCOVERING EARTH'S TIME MACHINE
1728–1787

James Hutton was born in 1726 in Scotland. James was a curious boy who loved to explore the countryside near his home. He would climb hills, study rocks, and wonder how the land was formed.

As a child, James noticed that rocks came in different layers and colors. He wondered how they got there and what they could tell us about the Earth's history. His parents encouraged his love for nature and learning.

When James grew up, he became a geologist. That means he studied the Earth and how it changes over time. One of James Hutton's biggest discoveries was about something called uniformitarianism. This is the idea that the same forces we see shaping the Earth today—like rain, wind, and erosion—have been acting for millions of years.

James spent a lot of time exploring rocks and cliffs. He observed how rivers carved valleys and how mountains were shaped over time. He wrote a famous book called *Theory of the Earth,* where he explained his ideas about how the Earth changes slowly, over a very long time.

James Hutton's discoveries changed how people thought about the Earth's history. Before him, many believed the Earth was only a few thousand years old. But James showed that it was much older and that its landscapes were shaped by processes that took millions of years.

Scientists still use James Hutton's principles to study geology and understand the planet we live on. James Hutton showed us that by exploring nature and asking questions, we can uncover amazing secrets about our world!

What's something in nature that you think might have taken a long time to form?

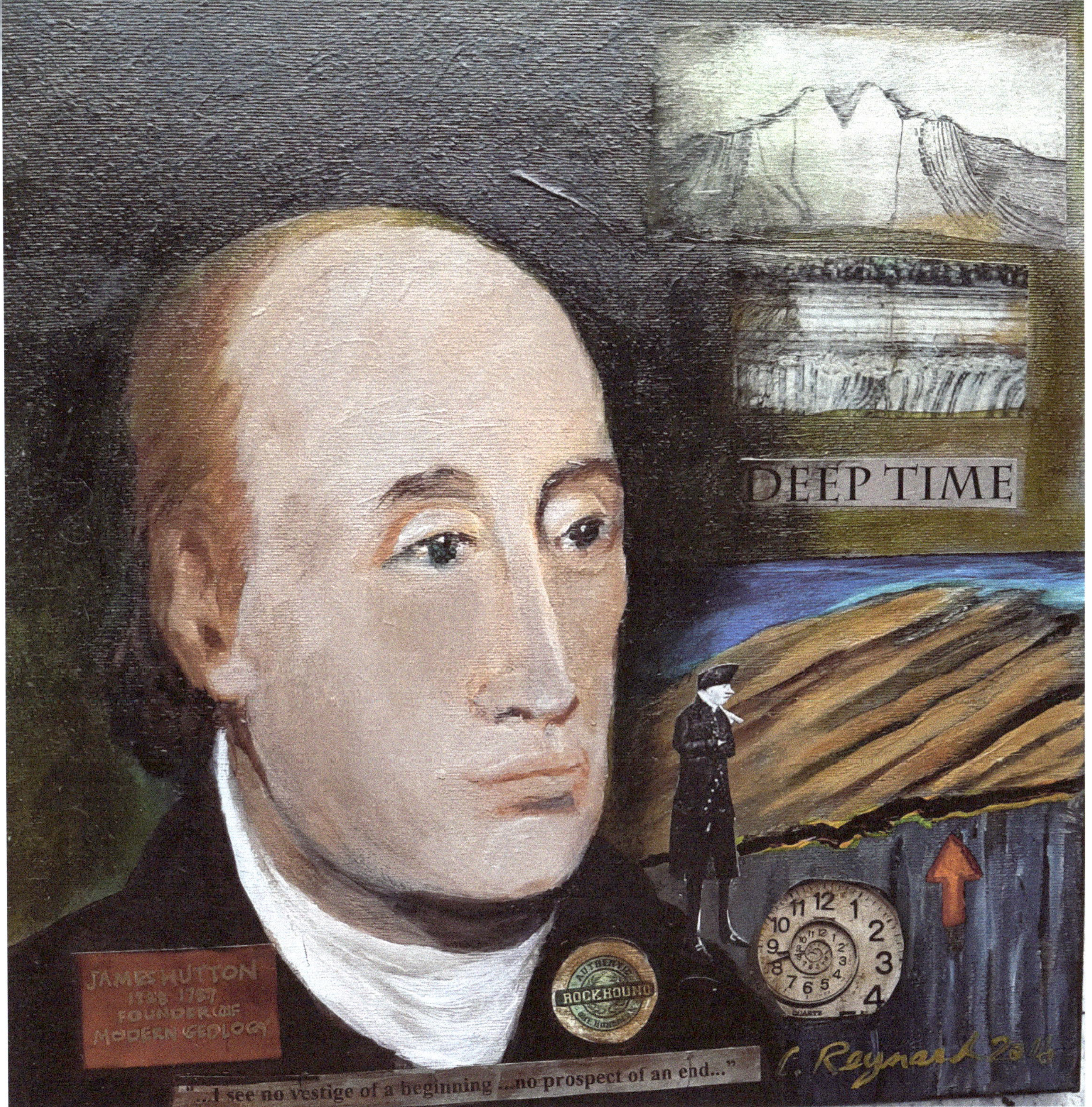
DEEP TIME
JAMES HUTTON
1726-1797
FOUNDER OF
MODERN GEOLOGY
ROCKHOUND
"...I see no vestige of a beginning ...no prospect of an end..."
C. Reynard 2016

RENÉ JUST HAÜY:
TRACING NATURE'S HIDDEN SHAPES
1743–1822

René Just Haüy was a scientist who lived a long time ago in France. René was a curious boy who loved to explore his surroundings, especially the forests and fields near his home in Saint-Just-en-Chaussée.

As a child, René was fascinated by rocks and minerals. He loved collecting shiny stones and pebbles, and he spent hours studying their different shapes and colors. His parents saw how much he loved nature and encouraged his interest in the world around him.

When René grew up, he became a scientist called a mineralogist. That means he studied rocks, minerals, and crystals. One of René Just Haüy's biggest discoveries was about the shape of crystals. Crystals are special because they form in a way that makes them have straight edges and flat faces, like a cube or a pyramid.

René noticed that no matter how big or small a crystal was, its shape was always the same. He figured out that this regular shape was because of the way atoms were arranged inside the crystal. This discovery helped scientists understand how minerals grow.

René Just Haüy wrote books and taught many students about crystals and minerals. He shared his knowledge with others who were interested in the wonders of nature. Many consider him the "Father of Modern Crystallography."

René Just Haüy's ideas are still really important in geology and chemistry today. Scientists still use his principles to study crystals and understand their properties.

René Just Haüy showed us that by exploring and studying nature, we can uncover amazing things about the shapes and structures in our world! Have you ever seen a crystal and wondered how it got its shape?

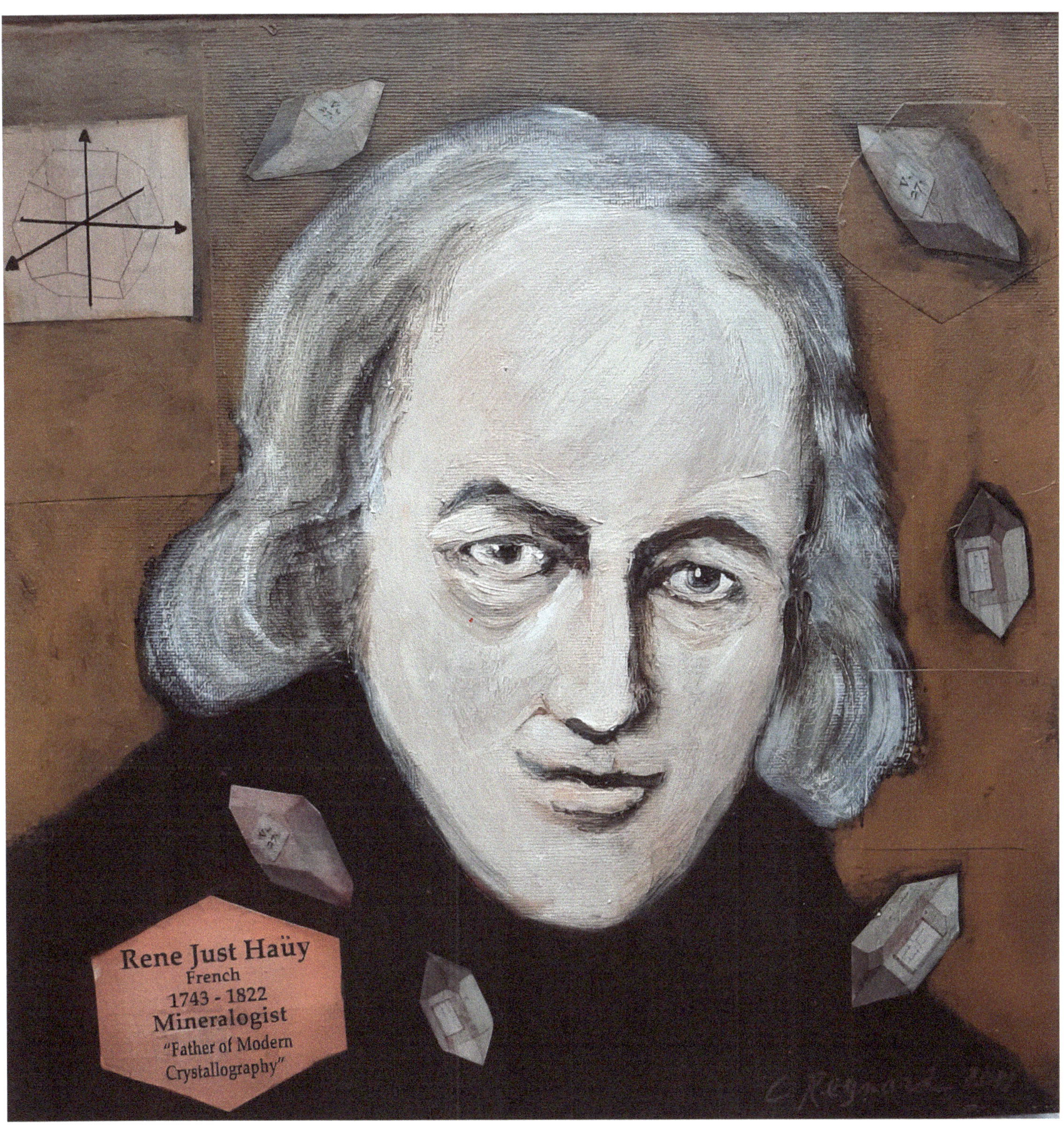

Rene Just Haüy
French
1743 - 1822
Mineralogist
"Father of Modern
Crystallography"

ADAM SEDGWICK:
LOOKING AT EARTH'S LAYERS
1785–1873

A scientist named Adam Sedgwick lived in the early 1800s in England. Adam was a curious boy who loved exploring the countryside near his home. He would wander through fields, climb hills, and look for interesting rocks and fossils.

As a child, Adam was fascinated by the different layers of rocks he found. He wondered how they formed and what they could tell us about the Earth's history. He was encouraged by his parents to learn more about rocks and minerals.

When Adam grew up, he became a geologist. That means he studied rocks and the Earth's crust to understand how they were made. One of Adam's biggest discoveries was about stratigraphy. This is the study of rock layers and how they are arranged.

Adam Sedgwick figured out that by looking at the order of rocks in different places, scientists could learn about the history of the Earth. He studied rocks in Wales and named a whole era of Earth's history, the Cambrian Period, after the Latin name for Wales: Cambria.

Adam also taught many students at the University of Cambridge, where he worked. He loved sharing his knowledge and passion for geology with others who were curious about the Earth. He may have even shared his knowledge with our next scientist, a fellow geologist named Sir Charles Lyell!

Scientists still use Adam Sedgwick's methods to study rock layers and understand how the Earth has changed over millions of years. Adam Sedgwick showed us that by exploring nature and asking questions, we can uncover amazing secrets about our planet!

Imagine you're exploring your favorite outdoor spot, finding rocks and fossils. Have you ever noticed different layers in the ground and wondered how they got there?

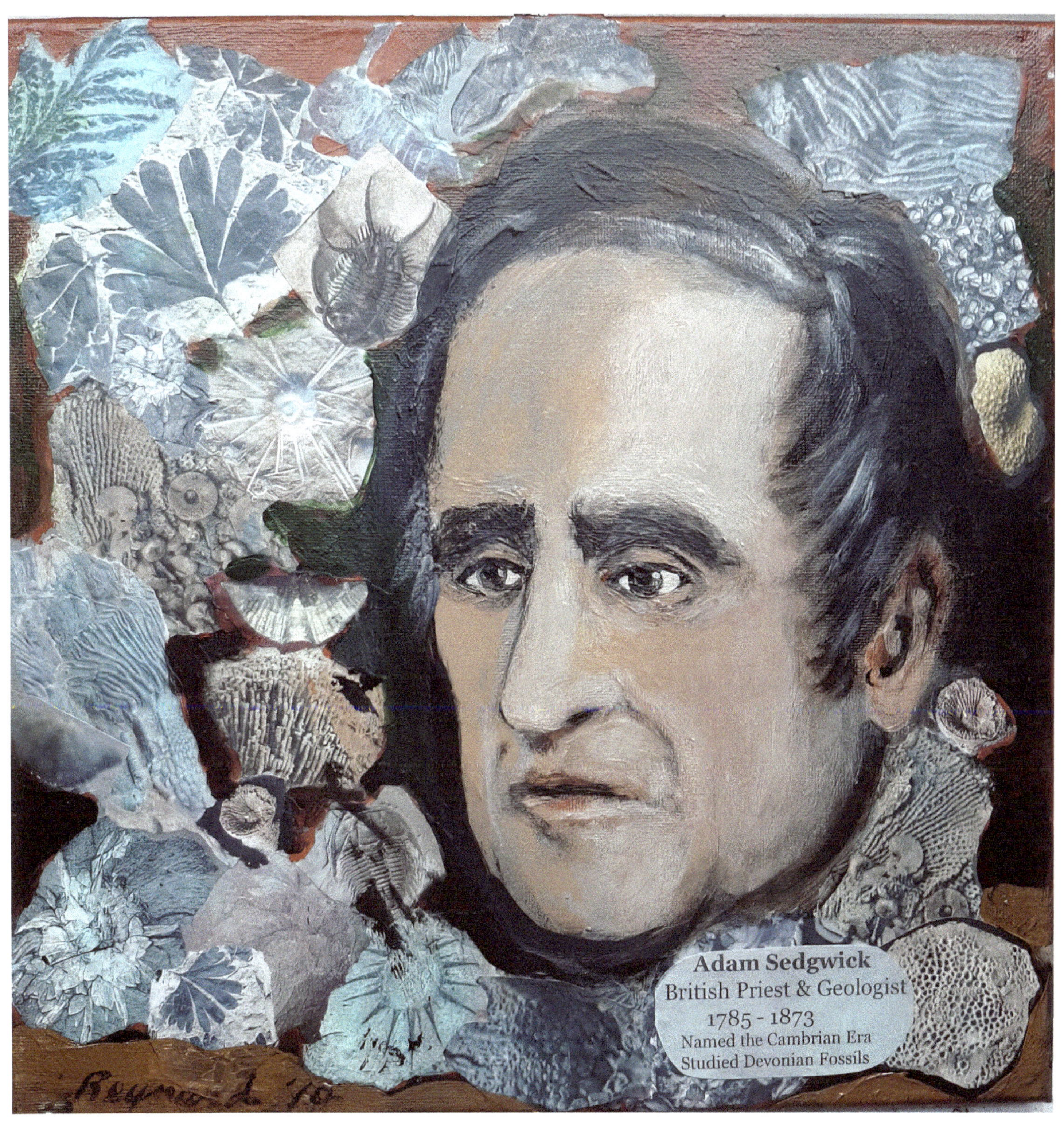

Adam Sedgwick
British Priest & Geologist
1785 - 1873
Named the Cambrian Era
Studied Devonian Fossils

SIR CHARLES LYELL: EXPLORING EARTH'S TIMELINE
1797–1875

Sir Charles Lyell was born in 1797 in Scotland. When he was almost two, his parents moved to Southampton, England. Charles was a curious boy who loved exploring the outdoors. He would go on walks with his family and marvel at the butterflies, rocks, and fossils he found along the way.

As a child, Charles was fascinated by how rocks formed and changed over time. He loved collecting fossils and studying the layers of earth he saw in cliffs and riverbanks. His parents saw how much he loved nature and encouraged him to learn more about it.

When Charles grew up, he became a geologist, studying the Earth and how it changes. One of Charles's biggest discoveries was about uniformitarianism, the idea that the processes shaping the Earth today, like erosion and volcanic activity, have been happening slowly over millions of years.

Charles Lyell traveled to many places, like Italy and France, to study rocks and fossils. He wrote a famous book called *Principles of Geology* where he explained his ideas. He showed how small changes over a long time could create big changes in the Earth's surface, like mountains and valleys.

Charles also studied how fossils could tell us about the history of life on Earth. He showed that fossils of ancient animals and plants could help us understand how different species evolved over time.

What's something in nature that you've seen change and wondered why?

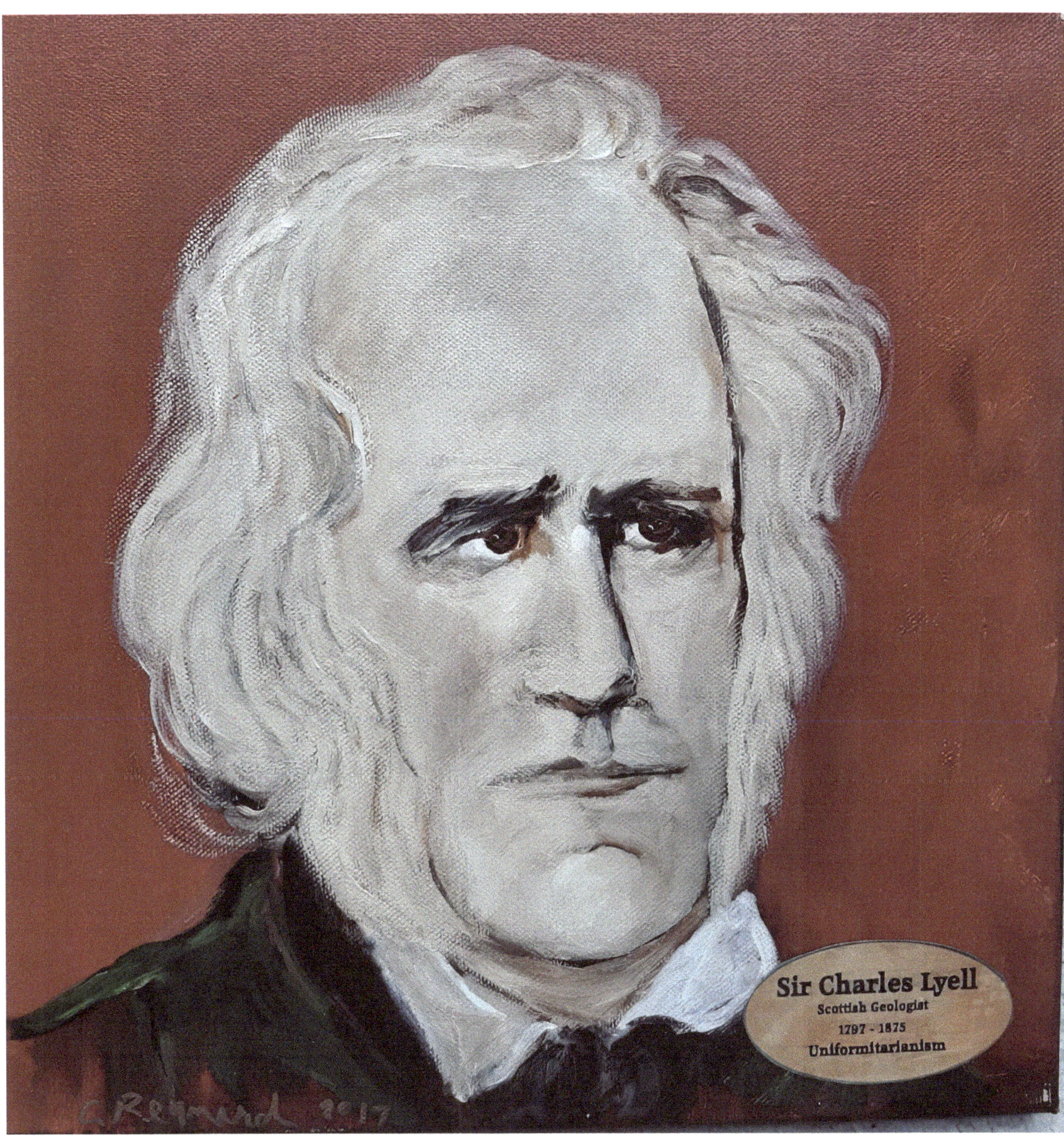

Sir Charles Lyell
Scottish Geologist
1797 - 1875
Uniformitarianism

JAMES HALL:
DISCOVERING PREHISTORIC TREASURES
1811–1898

James Hall was born in 1811 in a town called Hingham in Massachusetts, USA. James was a curious boy who loved to explore the outdoors, especially the rocky shores, hills, and woods of his hometown.

James was fascinated by the different types of rocks he found, from smooth river stones to jagged pieces of granite. His parents noticed how much he enjoyed collecting rocks and encouraged his interest in nature.

When James grew up, he became a New York state geologist, which means he studied rocks and the Earth. One of his biggest discoveries was about how rocks form and change over time. He studied fossils, too—those are ancient remains of plants and animals found in rocks. By studying fossils, James learned about creatures that lived long before people did!

James Hall also figured out that layers of rock can tell us a lot about Earth's history. Just like pages in a big book, each layer of rock holds stories about what happened in the past. He traveled to different places in America to study these rock layers and wrote many books to share what he learned with other scientists. Geologists today still use his ideas to understand how the Earth has changed over millions of years.

Have you ever found a fossil or something old and wondered what it used to be?

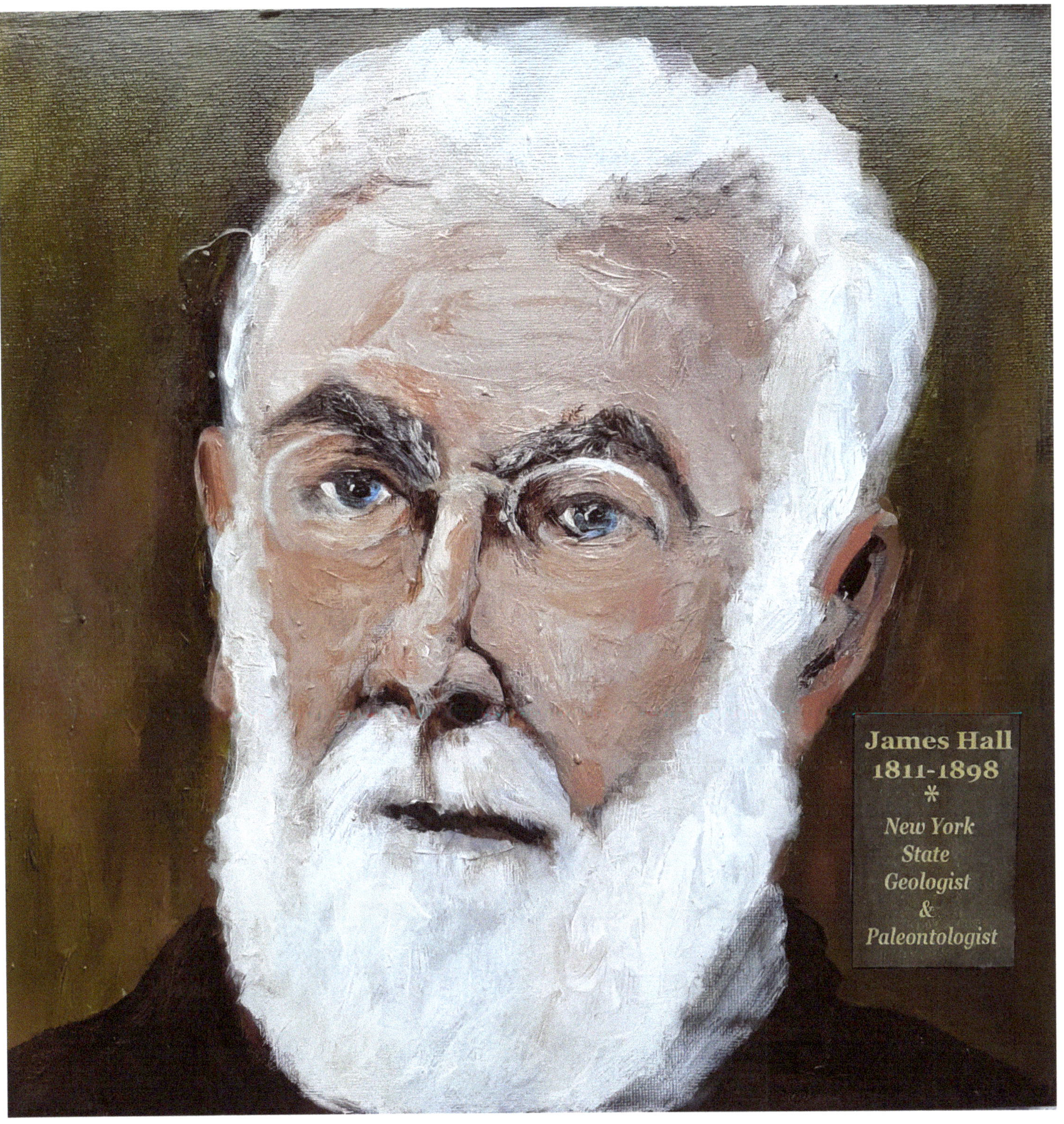
James Hall
1811-1898
*
New York
State
Geologist
&
Paleontologist

JAMES ORTON:
EXPLORING EARTH'S STORY THROUGH FOSSILS
1830–1877

As a child, James Orton loved to explore and discover new things about the world around him. When he was young, he spent hours watching the ants crawl around in his backyard. But what really showed he was going to be a scientist was when he found a special rock near a river. He took it home and asked his dad to help him figure out what kind of rock it was. His dad said it was a fossil, which is a rock with ancient remains of plants and animals in it. Fossils show us what plants and animals looked like long ago. James was so excited that he decided he wanted to learn more about rocks and fossils when he grew up.

As James got older, he kept exploring and learning. He read lots of books about rocks, fossils, and animals. He even started writing down all the interesting things he learned in a notebook. When he grew up, he went to college and studied geology, which is the science of rocks and fossils. James traveled around the world to find and study rocks and fossils. He wrote books about what he discovered and taught others about the amazing things he found at Vassar College in Poughkeepsie, New York.

If you could explore any place on Earth, where would you go and what would you hope to discover?

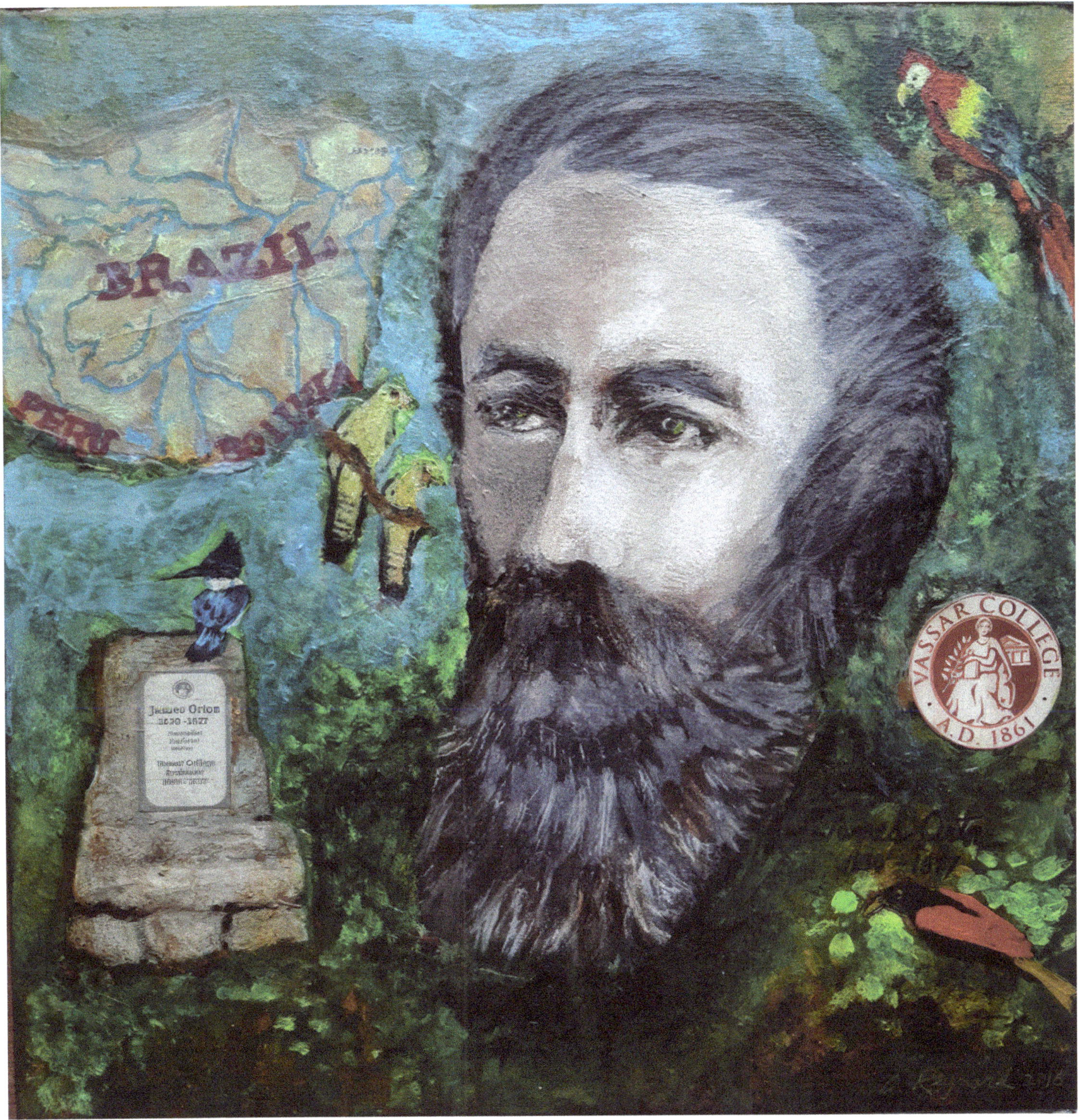

BRAZIL
PERU
BOLIVIA
James Orton
VASSAR COLLEGE
A.D. 1861

VICTOR GOLDSCHMIDT:
DISCOVERING TEMPERATURE+ PRESSURE = MINERAL
1888–1947

Victor Moritz Goldschmidt was born in 1888 in Switzerland. Victor loved playing with rocks and minerals as a little boy. He would collect them and try to understand why they looked different and where they came from.

As a kid, Victor was curious about how the Earth was made. He liked to dig in the dirt and find different kinds of stones. His parents saw how much he loved rocks and minerals, and they encouraged him to learn more about them.

When Victor grew up, he became a geologist. He studied how rocks form and what they're made of. He wanted to know why some rocks were shiny, like gold, and others were rough, like sandstone.

One of Victor's biggest discoveries was about how minerals form. He figured out that the temperature and pressure deep inside the Earth can change rocks into different minerals. This helped scientists understand more about how our planet works and how minerals are created.

Victor Goldschmidt also studied elements. These elements are like tiny building blocks that are combined to make everything! Victor investigated how elements move through rocks and how they can change over time. He wrote many books and papers to share his discoveries with other scientists around the world, and they continue to influence geology today. What's something around you that you think might have interesting elements to discover?

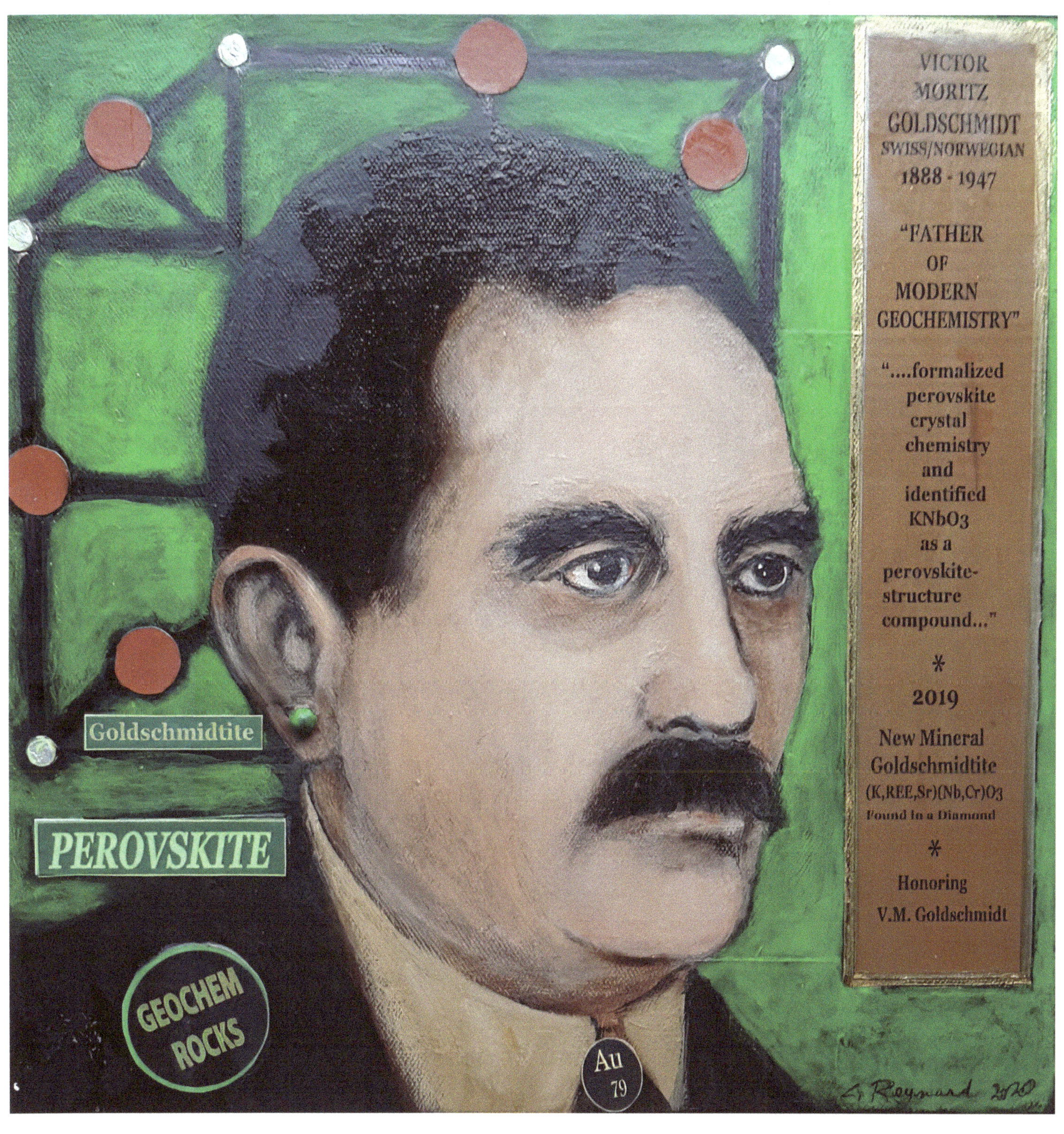
Goldschmidtite
PEROVSKITE
GEOCHEM ROCKS
Au 79
VICTOR MORITZ GOLDSCHMIDT
SWISS/NORWEGIAN
1888 - 1947

"FATHER OF MODERN GEOCHEMISTRY"

"....formalized perovskite crystal chemistry and identified KNbO3 as a perovskite-structure compound..."

*
2019
New Mineral
Goldschmidtite
(K,REE,Sr)(Nb,Cr)O3
Found in a Diamond
*
Honoring
V.M. Goldschmidt

G. Reynard 2020

VIRGIL COLE:
UNEARTHING ANCIENT SEAS AND FOSSILS
1897–1984

Virgil B. Cole (Mrs. Reynard's dad!) was like a super-smart treasure hunter who searched for oil deep underground and even discovered a dinosaur skeleton. Imagine someone who used special tools and maps to find hidden treasures beneath the earth. That was Virgil!

Virgil was born on August 14, 1897, in a small farmhouse in Missouri. He loved learning about the land and decided to study agriculture at the University of Missouri. His studies were interrupted when he served in the army, first on the Mexican border in 1916 and then as a medical corpsman in France during World War I. While in France, Virgil explored tunnels, trenches, and caverns, which sparked his interest in geology.

After returning from the war, Virgil switched his focus to geology and earned a master's degree in 1923. That same year, he got a summer job with the Gypsy Oil Company, which later became the Gulf Oil Corporation. What was supposed to be a temporary job turned into a thirty-year career!

Virgil was known for his amazing memory and knowledge about geology. People even called him "a walking computer" because he could remember so much geological data. He made a famous map called the "Configuration of the Precambrian Surface in the State of Kansas," which helped other geologists understand the underground layers of the state.

During his career, Virgil did many exciting things. He mapped surface rocks on the Navajo Reservation and worked on finding places to drill for oil. One time, he and his team drilled a well that provided fresh water for the Navajo Nation.

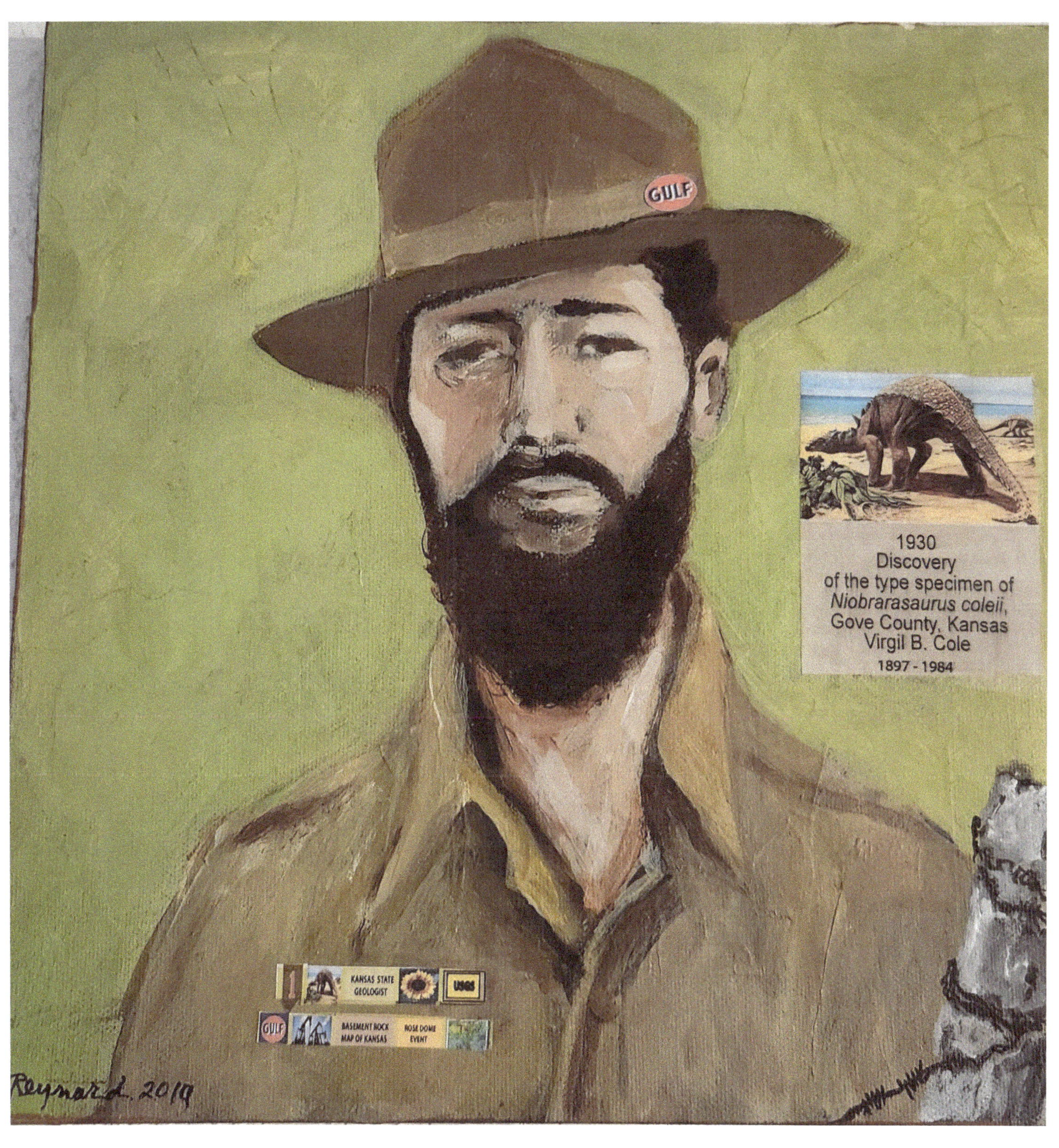
GULF
1930
Discovery
of the type specimen of
Niobrarasaurus coleii,
Gove County, Kansas
Virgil B. Cole
1897 - 1984
KANSAS STATE GEOLOGIST
USGS
GULF
BASEMENT ROCK MAP OF KANSAS
ROSE DOME EVENT
Reynard. 2019

After retiring from the Gulf Oil Corporation, Virgil continued to help others as a consultant for the Kansas Geological Survey. He was admired and respected for his work and contributions to geology.

And here's the fun part: while searching for oil, Virgil discovered a dinosaur fossil! It was like finding a giant, ancient puzzle buried in the earth. This incredible find made him feel like a true explorer. There is a photo of what that dinosaur may have looked like on the back cover of this book.

Virgil B. Cole was like a detective, solving the mysteries of where oil was hidden under the earth and finding ancient dinosaur bones. He showed us that with curiosity and hard work, we can uncover amazing things that help make our world a better place. So, the next time you see a car driving or read about dinosaurs, think of Virgil and his incredible adventures!

If you could explore underground like Virgil B. Cole did, searching for hidden treasures or fossils, what would you hope to discover and why?

CHAPTER 3

MAPPERS OF EARTH ON THE MOVE

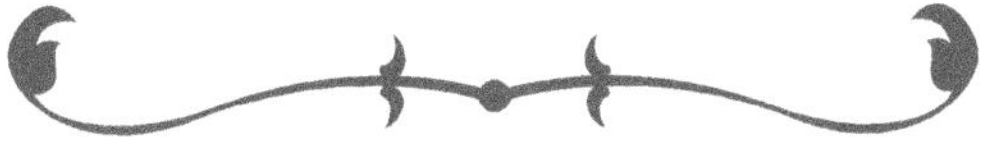

JAMES DANA:
EXPLORING EARTH'S GEOLOGICAL MARVELS
1813–1895

James D. Dana was a really cool scientist from a long time ago. He was born in 1813 in the United States. When he was growing up in western New York, he loved exploring nature and collecting rocks and shells. His parents saw how curious he was about the world around him. His high school science teacher encouraged his scientific mind.

James Dana grew up to be a famous geologist. He studied rocks, minerals, and the Earth's crust. He even went on a big adventure sailing around the world on a ship called the USS Vincennes. Can you imagine exploring the oceans like that?

One of his biggest discoveries was figuring out how volcanoes work. He studied lava and volcanic rocks to understand how they form and why volcanoes erupt. That was a huge deal because it helped scientists understand more about the Earth's structure.

James Dana wrote lots of books and papers about geology, so he taught a lot of people about rocks and minerals. He loved sharing his knowledge with others.

Even though he lived a long time ago, we still learn from his work today. He showed us how amazing the Earth is and why we should take care of it. James D. Dana was like a rock star of geology!

Have you ever collected rocks or minerals and wondered how they got there and what they were made of?

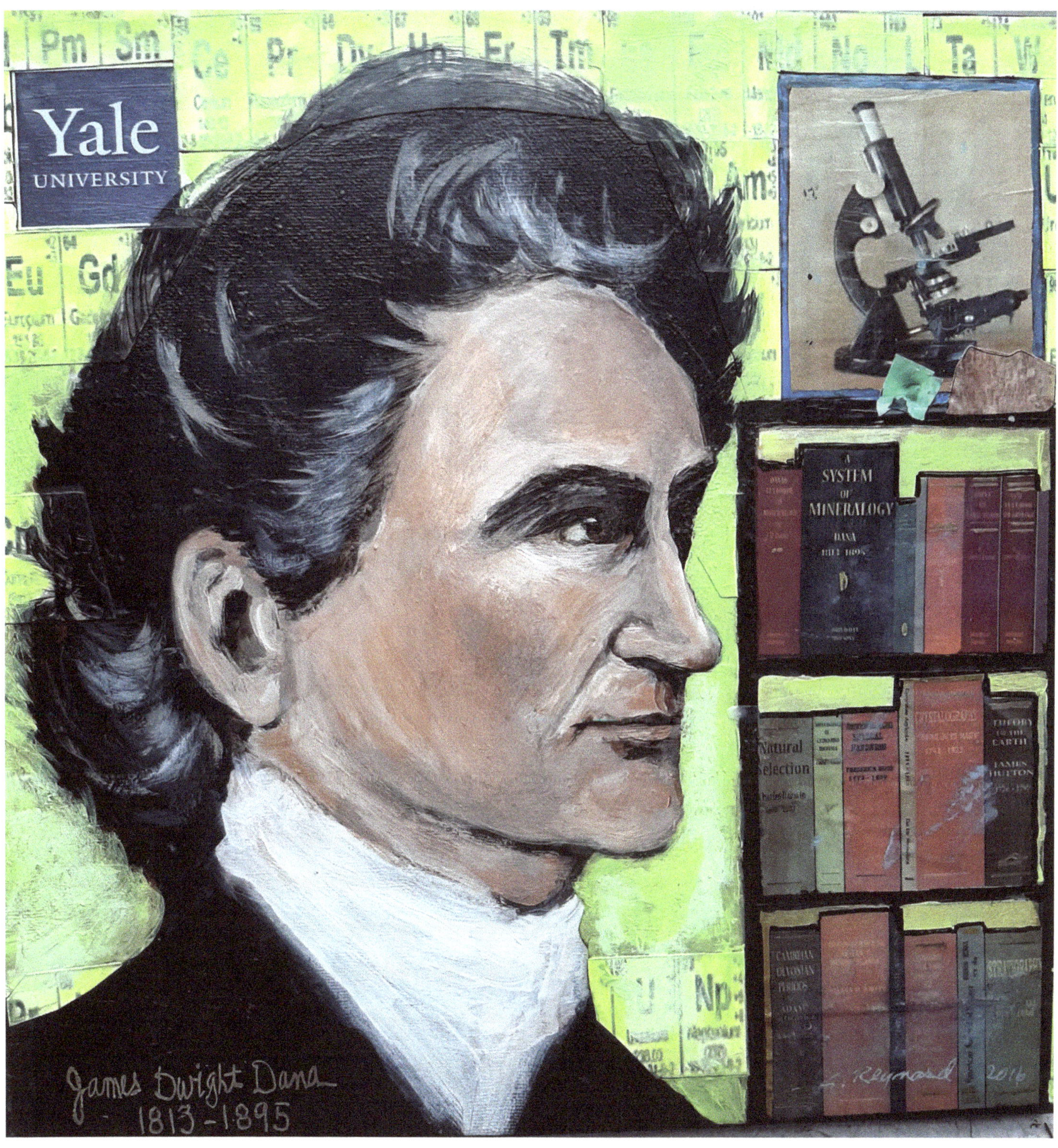

Yale
UNIVERSITY
A
SYSTEM
of
MINERALOGY
DANA
Natural
Selection
THEORY
OF THE
EARTH
JAMES
HUTTON
CAMBRIAN
DEVONIAN
PERIODS
James Dwight Dana
1813 - 1895
L. Reynaud 2016

ALFRED WEGENER:
PIECING TOGETHER EARTH'S DRIFTING PUZZLE
1880–1930

Alfred Wegener loved figuring out puzzles about our Earth. Imagine looking at a map and wondering why the shapes of the continents seem to fit together like a jigsaw puzzle. That's exactly what Alfred did!

He came up with a big idea called continental drift. He thought that a long, long time ago, all the continents were stuck together in one huge land, which he called Pangaea. Over millions of years, Pangaea slowly broke apart, and the pieces moved to where they are now.

To prove his idea, Alfred looked at different clues. He noticed that the shapes of some continents, like South America and Africa, looked like they could fit together. He also found fossils of the same plants and animals on continents that are now really far apart. And when he looked at certain rocks and mountains, he saw that they matched up when you put the continents together.

Not everyone believed Alfred at first. Many scientists thought he was wrong. But Alfred didn't give up. He kept studying and finding more evidence to support his idea. A fellow scientist named Alex du Toit agreed with him. His story is up next.

We know now that Alfred Wegener was right! Scientists have discovered more about how the Earth works, something called plate tectonics, which explains how the continents move around.

So, Alfred Wegener was a master at solving the puzzle of how the continents move and change over time. His idea helped us understand that the Earth's surface is always changing, just like pieces of a giant puzzle!

Have you noticed any clues in your environment that might show how things have changed over time?

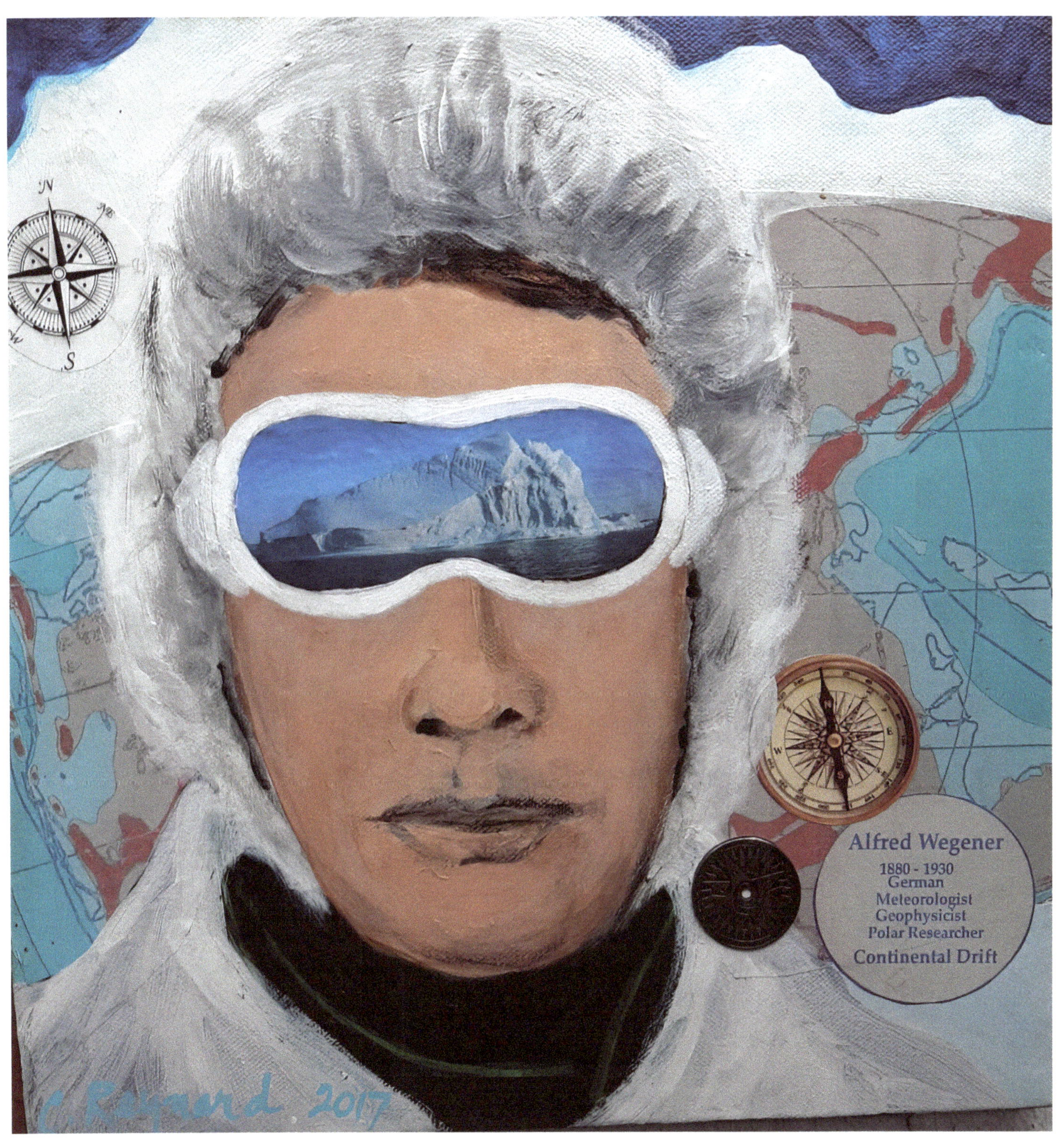
N
Alfred Wegener
1880 - 1930
German
Meteorologist
Geophysicist
Polar Researcher
Continental Drift
C. Rognvald 2017

ALEXANDER DU TOIT:
JOURNEYING TO THE LAND OF DINOSAURS
1878–1948

Alexander du Toit was born in South Africa in 1878. Alexander, who was also called Alex, was a curious boy who loved exploring the rugged landscapes near his home. He would hike through mountains and valleys, marveling at the strange rocks he found.

As a child, Alex was fascinated by dinosaurs and ancient creatures. He loved reading books about them and dreaming of finding fossils himself. His parents encouraged his interest in the Earth's history.

When Alex grew up, he became a geologist, studying rocks and the Earth's crust. Alex and a fellow scientist, Alfred Wegener, agreed that millions of years ago, the continents were actually connected in a supercontinent called Pangaea. Alex and Alfred noticed that the shapes of continents, like Africa and South America, looked like they could fit together like pieces of a puzzle. Over time, these pieces drifted apart to where they are now. This discovery helped scientists understand how the Earth's surface changes over millions of years.

Alex also studied fossils to learn about the plants and animals that lived long ago. He found fossils of ancient reptiles and plants that helped scientists piece together the story of life on Earth.

Alex du Toit wrote books and taught students about his discoveries. He loved sharing his passion for geology with others who were curious about the Earth's past. Scientists still use his theories to study how continents move and how Earth's landscapes change. A crater on Mars was named du Toit in honor of Alex's contributions to science!

What's something you've learned about geography or maps that surprised you? Did you share your idea with a friend?

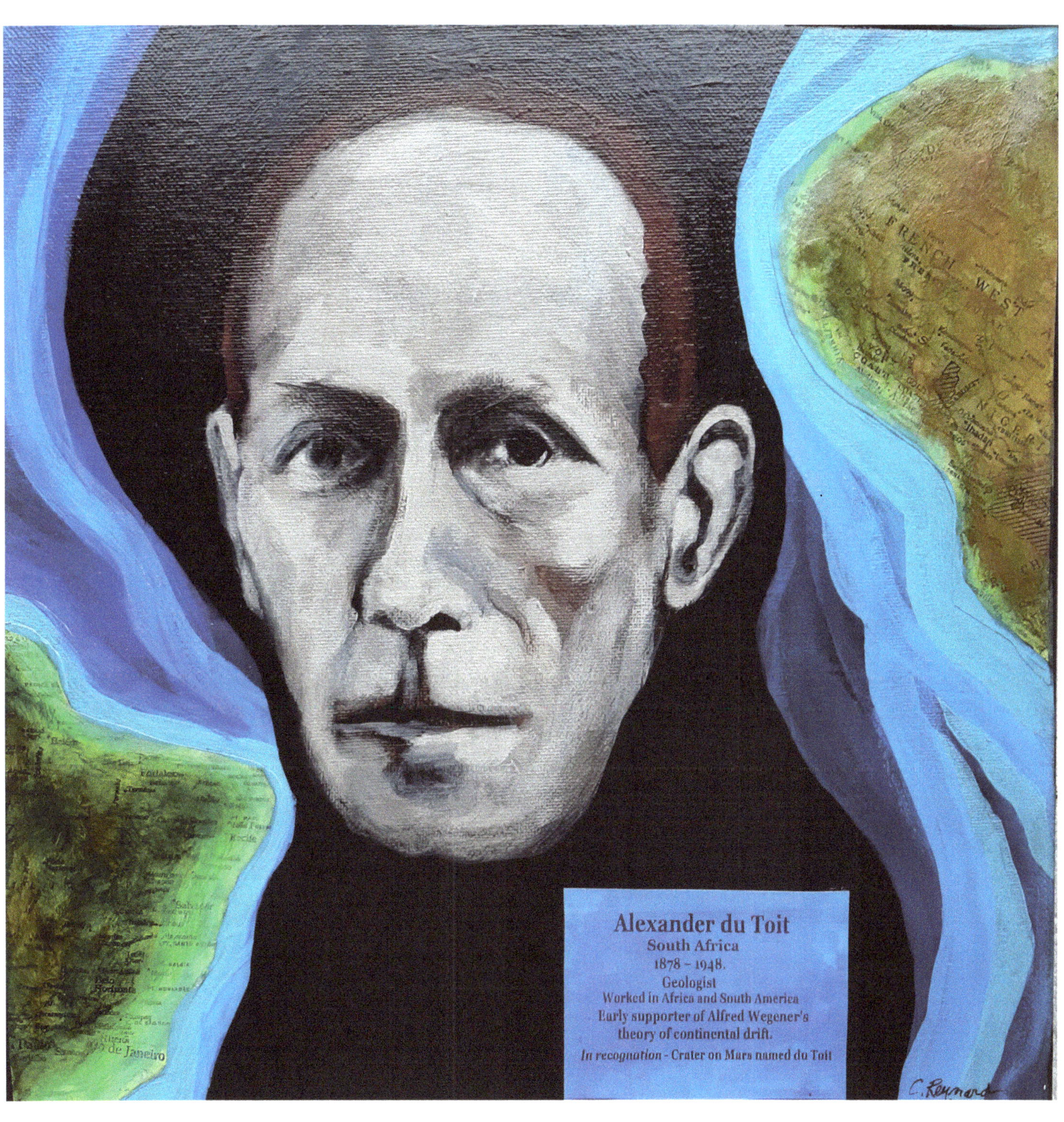
Alexander du Toit
South Africa
1878 - 1948.
Geologist
Worked in Africa and South America
Early supporter of Alfred Wegener's
theory of continental drift.
In recognition - Crater on Mars named du Toit
C. Reynard

HARRY HESS:
EXPLORING THE DEEP SECRETS OF EARTH'S OCEANS
1906–1969

Harry Hess was a scientist who lived in the twentieth century and was interested in what's under the ocean. He was born in New York in 1906 and grew up loving rocks and exploring nature.

One of his big discoveries was something called seafloor spreading. This is the theory that the ocean floor is moving and spreading apart over time. Hess figured out that new ocean crust forms at underwater mountains called mid-ocean ridges, and then it moves away from there.

Hess was influenced by Alfred Wegener, who came up with the theory of continental drift. Wegener said that the continents move slowly over millions of years, and this idea fascinated Hess. He thought about how the seafloor spreading could fit with Wegener's theory, and it helped scientists understand how Earth's crust changes.

Hess didn't just stay in a lab; he went on ships to explore the ocean floor and find evidence for his ideas. His discoveries changed how we understand the Earth's surface.

Harry Hess was like a detective of the ocean floor who used his love for rocks and nature to uncover how our planet works in a whole new way! What about the Earth would you like to learn more about?

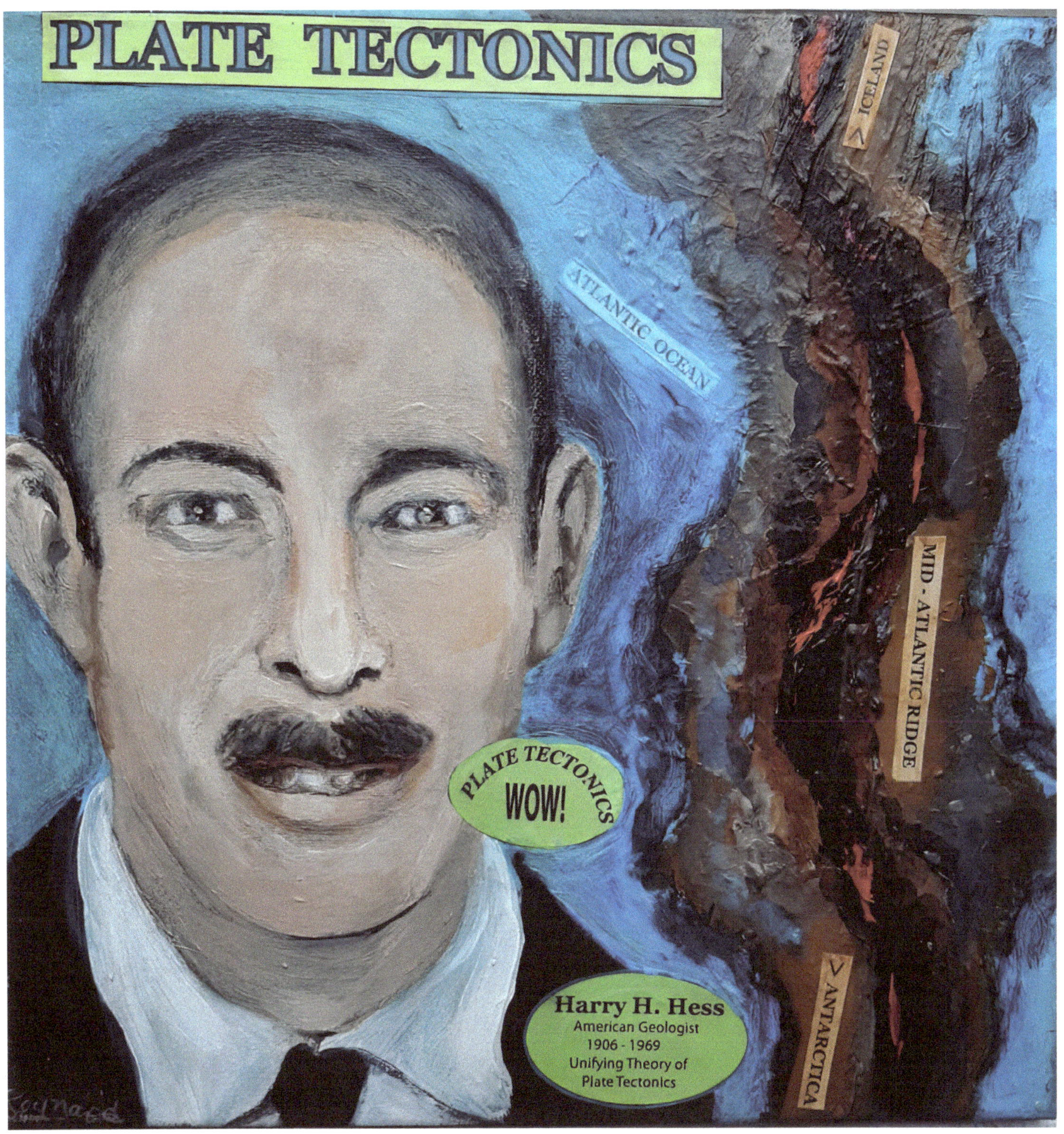

PLATE TECTONICS
ICELAND
ATLANTIC OCEAN
MID - ATLANTIC RIDGE
ANTARCTICA
PLATE TECTONICS
WOW!
Harry H. Hess
American Geologist
1906 - 1969
Unifying Theory of
Plate Tectonics

J. Tuzo Wilson:
Adding the Heat to Earth's Puzzle
1908–1993

There was a scientist named J. Tuzo Wilson, who was born in 1908 in Canada. Tuzo, as he liked to be called, was a curious boy who loved exploring the outdoors. He would climb trees, look for fossils, and wonder about how the Earth worked.

As a child, Tuzo was fascinated by mountains and volcanoes. He would read books about them and dream about visiting faraway places with amazing landscapes. His family saw how much he loved nature, and they encouraged him to learn more about it.

When Tuzo grew up, he became a geologist and a geophysicist. That means he studied the Earth and how it changes over time. One of Tuzo's biggest discoveries was about plate tectonics. Other geologists were studying this, too. This is the idea that the Earth's surface is made up of giant pieces, like a jigsaw puzzle, that move around very slowly.

Tuzo Wilson learned about Alfred Wegener and Harry Hess and their observations. Tuzo figured out that these plates move because of the heat inside the Earth. He studied how mountains form when plates collide and how earthquakes happen when plates rub against each other.

Tuzo loved to travel to different countries to study mountains and volcanoes up close. He wrote many books and taught students about his discoveries so that they could learn from him, too.

Scientists still use Tuzo Wilson's theories to study earthquakes, volcanoes, and even how continents move over millions of years.

Tuzo Wilson showed us that by exploring, asking questions, and sharing observations about Earth with other scientists, we can discover amazing things about the world we live in. How can you explore, ask questions, and share your ideas with family and friends?

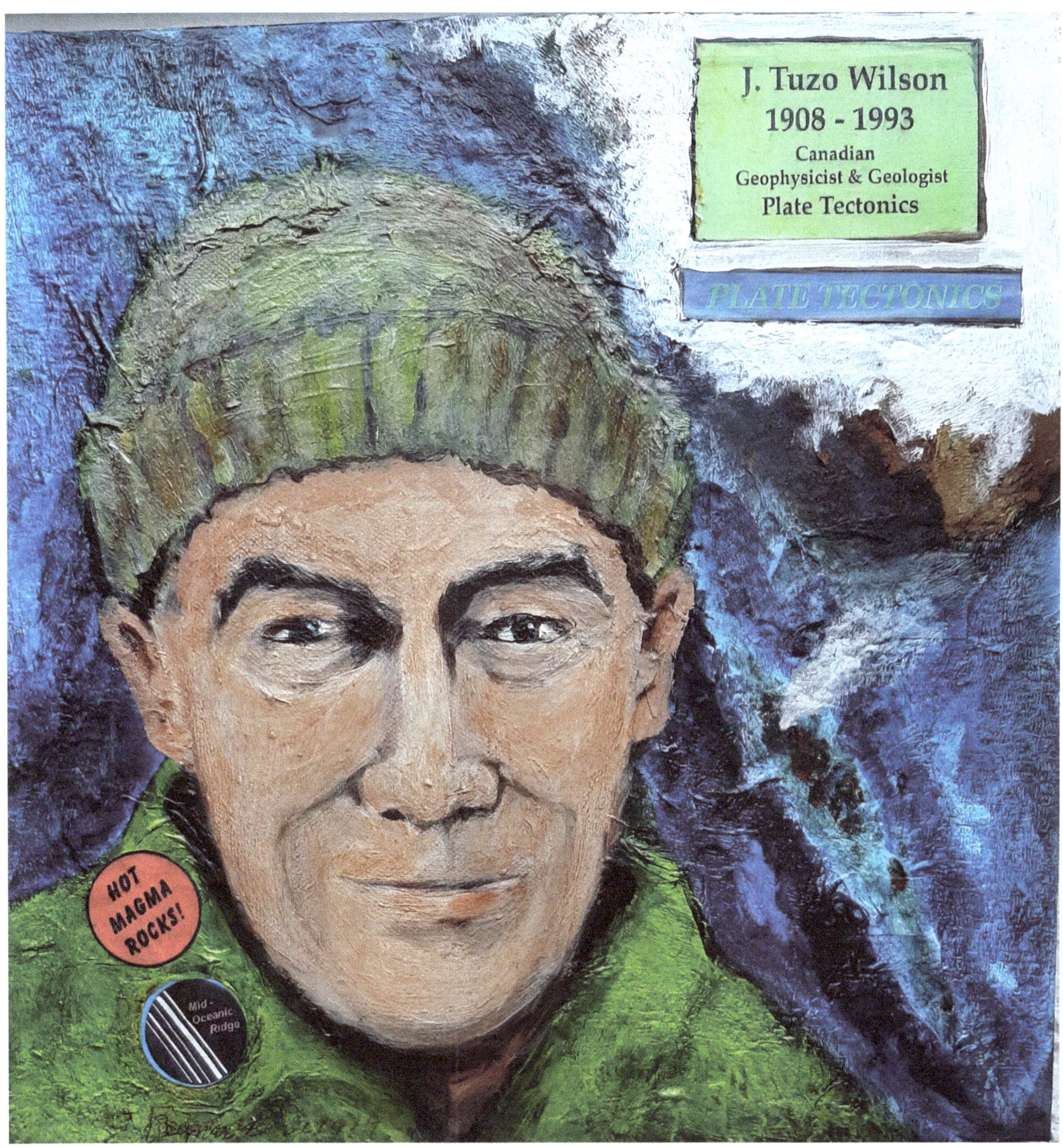
J. Tuzo Wilson
1908 - 1993
Canadian
Geophysicist & Geologist
Plate Tectonics
PLATE TECTONICS
HOT MAGMA ROCKS!
Mid - Oceanic Ridge

MARIE THARP:
MAPPING THE DEPTHS OF THE EARTH'S SECRETS
1920–2006

Marie Tharp loved exploring the mysteries of the ocean. Imagine someone who takes lots of clues and pieces them together to make a big, beautiful picture of something no one has ever seen before. That was Marie!

Marie was a geologist and cartographer, which means she studied rocks and made maps. But she didn't make just any maps; she made the first detailed maps of the ocean floor! Before her work, people thought the ocean floor was flat and boring. Marie discovered that it was actually full of mountains, valleys, and deep trenches.

She worked with lots of data from ships that measured the depth of the ocean at different places. Using this information, she carefully drew maps that showed what the ocean floor looked like. One of her biggest discoveries was a giant underwater mountain range called the Mid-Atlantic Ridge. This ridge is part of a huge system of mountains that go all around the Earth under the oceans.

Marie's maps helped scientists understand how continents move and supported the theories of Alfred Wegener, Harry Hess, and Tuzo Wilson about plate tectonics. She showed by her data from ships that the ocean floor is spreading apart. This helps explain why continents drift across the Earth's surface.

Even though some people didn't agree with her at first, Marie kept working hard and, eventually, everyone saw that she and other scientists were right. Her work changed how we understand our planet and the oceans.

Marie Tharp uncovered the hidden landscape under the ocean. She showed us the importance of looking closely at clues and believing in your discoveries!

Marie Tharp mapped the ocean floor and discovered the Mid-Atlantic Ridge. How does her exploration of the oceans relate to your curiosity about the natural world?

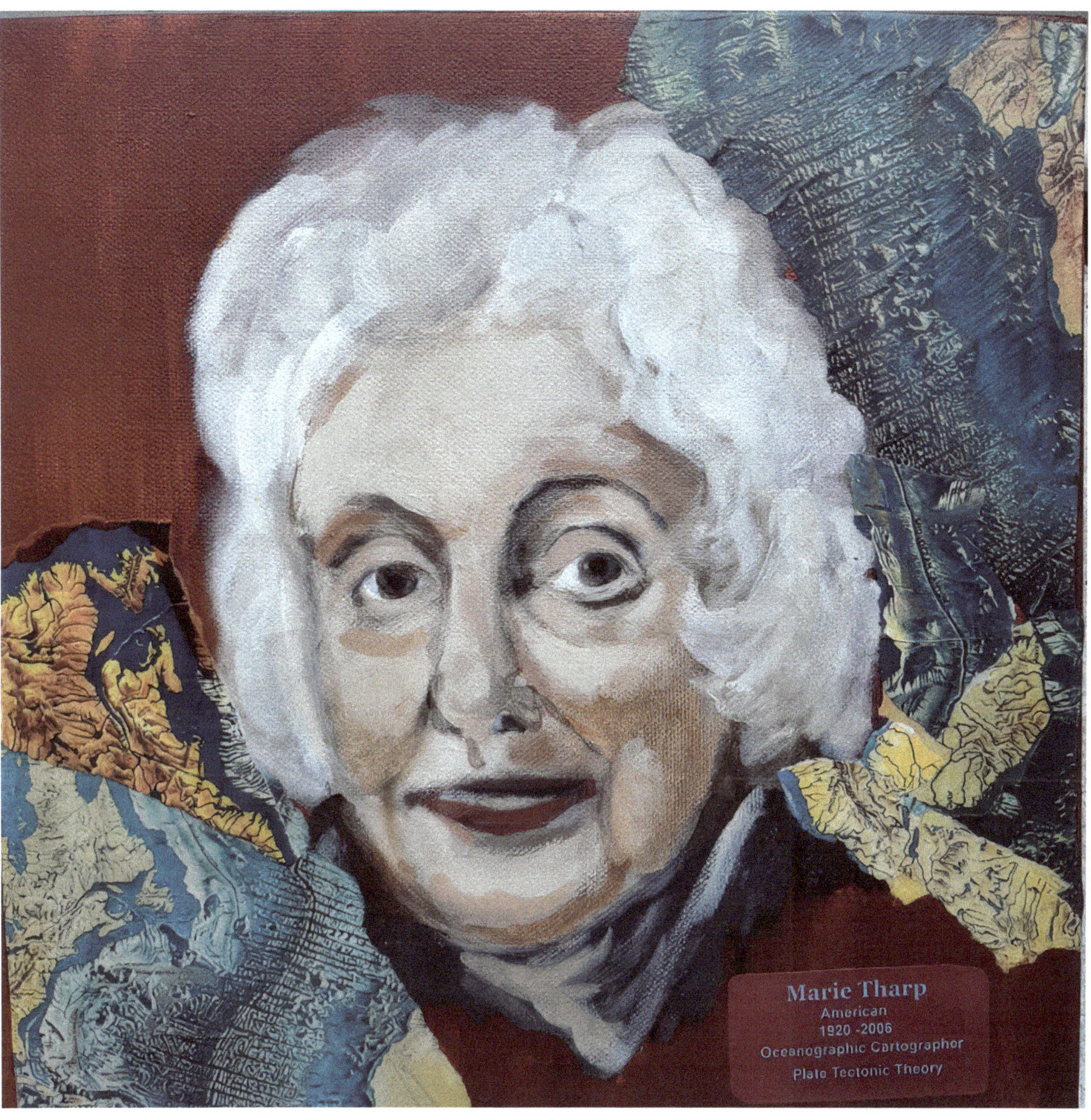

Marie Tharp
American
1920 -2006
Oceanographic Cartographer
Plate Tectonic Theory

CHAPTER 4

COMMUNICATORS OF SCIENTIFIC INFORMATION

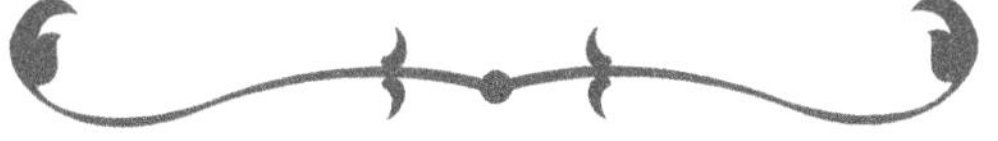

IBN AL-HAYTHAM: ILLUMINATING THE SECRETS OF LIGHT, VISION, AND THE SCIENTIFIC METHOD
965–1040

Ibn al-Haytham, also known as Alhazen, was a very clever person who was born in Basra, Iraq and loved exploring and discovering new things about the world.

He was especially curious about light, so he did many experiments with mirrors and lenses to learn about it. He had a method where he would first observe something and then guess what would happen if he changed something. After making the change, he would do the experiment again and observe what happened. He repeated this process many times to figure out what caused the changes he saw.

Today, scientists use this same method to learn about the world. We call it the scientific method. While Sir Francis Bacon is often credited as the father of the scientific method, Alhazen's ideas laid the foundation for it.

One of his most amazing discoveries was that light travels in straight lines. He used this idea to explain how we see things and why shadows appear when something blocks light. He wrote a book called *Kitab al-Manazir*, or *"Book of Optics,"* where he explained these ideas.

Ibn al-Haytham also invented something called the camera obscura. It is a box with a small hole in it. When light shines through the hole, it creates an upside-down picture of what's outside the box. This was the very first type of camera!

Ibn al-Haytham was like a wizard of light, using his experiments and inventions to unlock the secrets of how we see the world around us. He inspires us to keep exploring and learning! How does experimenting with light and colors help you understand the world around you?

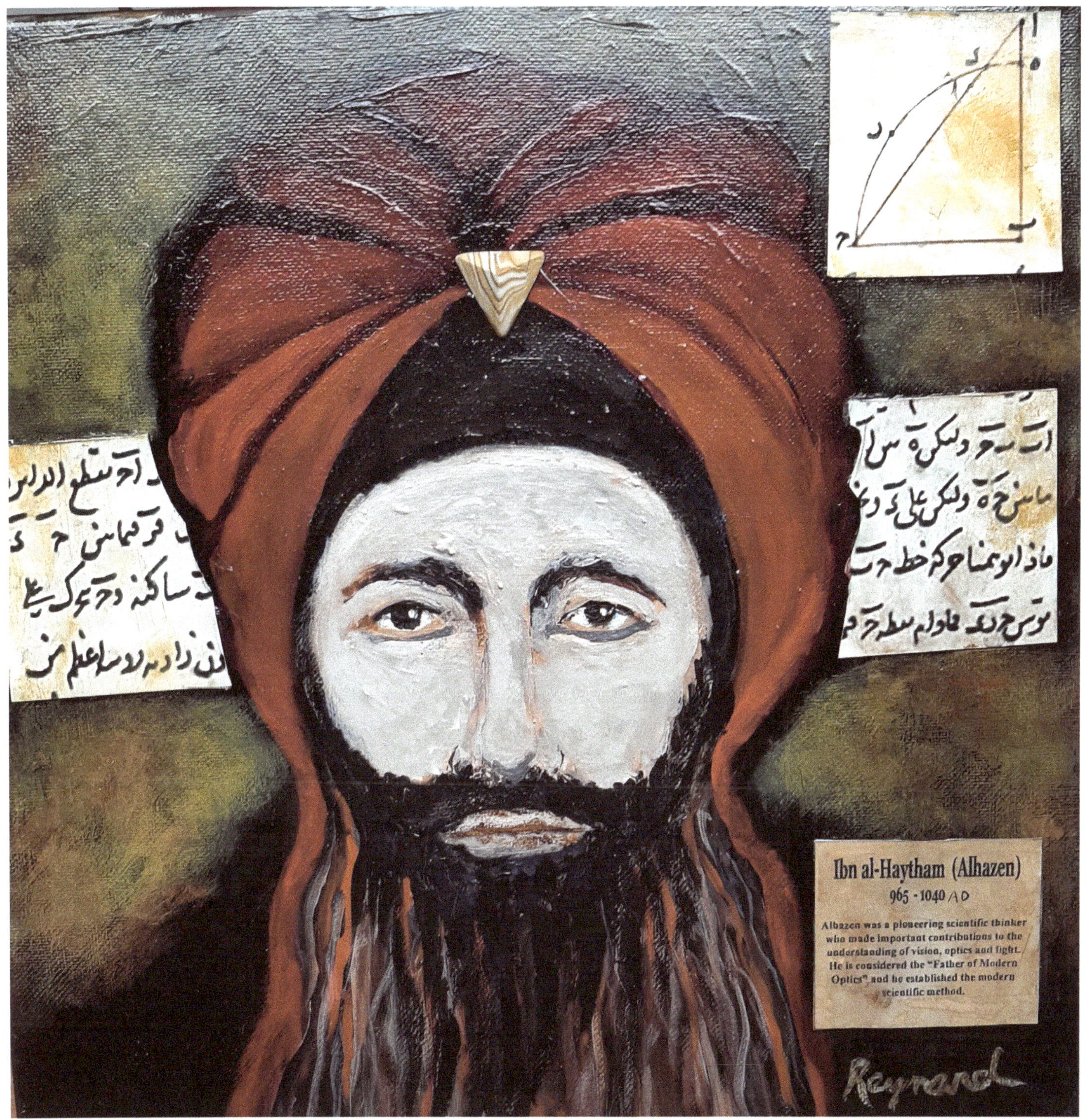
Ibn al-Haytham (Alhazen)
965 - 1040 AD
Alhazen was a pioneering scientific thinker
who made important contributions to the
understanding of vision, optics and light.
He is considered the "Father of Modern
Optics" and he established the modern
scientific method.
Reynard

LEONARDO DA VINCI:
MASTERING ART AND INVENTION
1452–1519

Leonardo da Vinci was an amazing person who lived in Italy during the fifteenth and sixteenth centuries. He was not just an artist but also a scientist and inventor.

As a child, Leonardo loved exploring nature and drawing everything he saw. It has been said that he had interesting habits, like writing backwards, spelling strangely, and not following through on projects. Today, we understand that these behaviors can all be characteristics of dyslexia and other learning differences. That didn't stop Leonardo!

He's most famous for his paintings, like the Mona Lisa and The Last Supper. But Leonardo was also really curious about how things worked. He studied birds to learn how they could fly and even designed a flying machine! He also drew detailed pictures of the human body to understand how it worked inside.

Leonardo da Vinci made so many discoveries that helped us understand science and art better. He showed us how detailed drawings could help scientists and artists learn new things. Even though he lived a long time ago, his ideas still inspire people all over the world today!

Like Leonardo da Vinci, do you enjoy drawing or building things? What's something in nature that you've drawn or built that reminds you of Leonardo's curiosity about how things work?

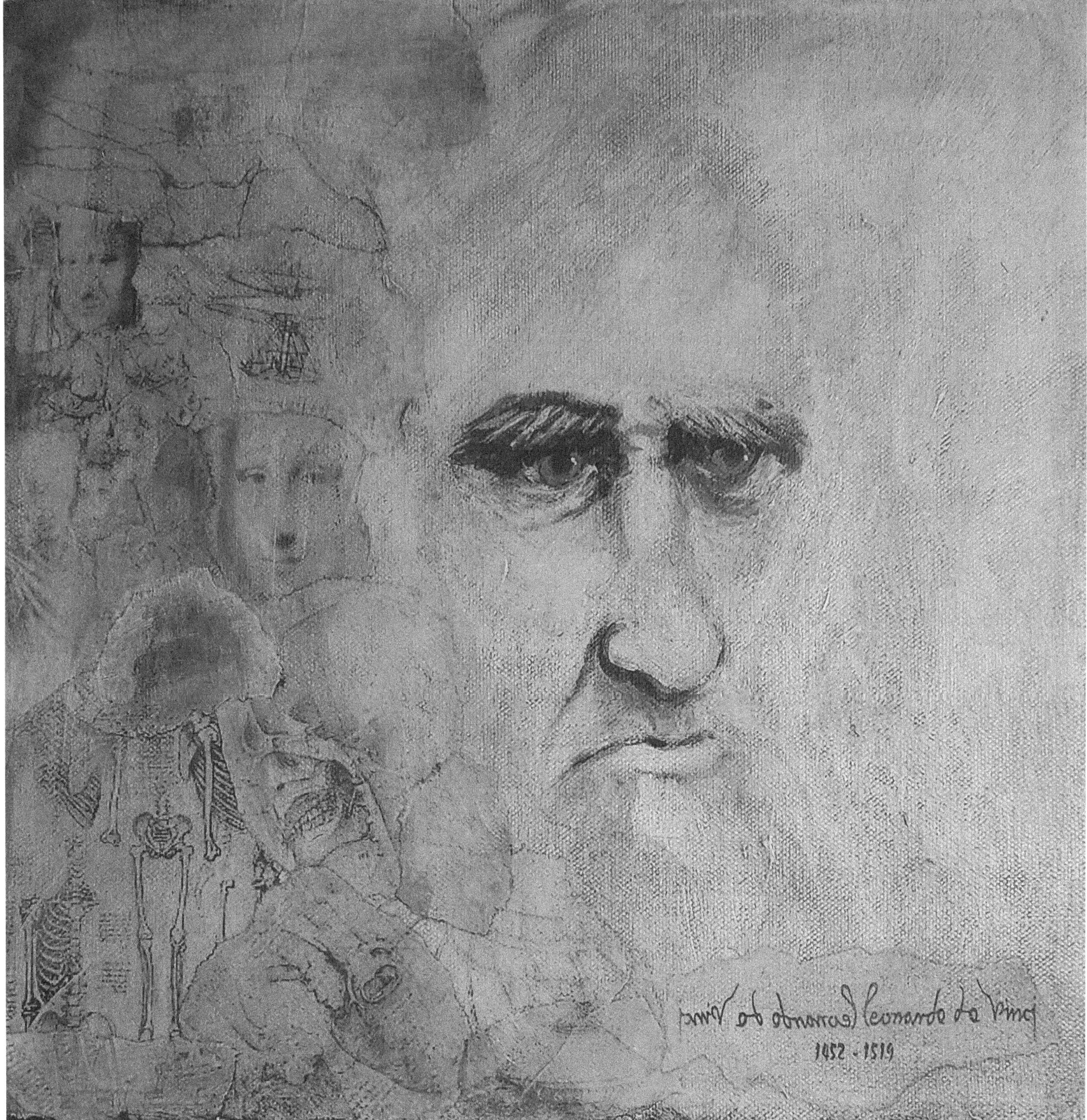
leonardo da Vinci
1452 - 1519

ANDERS CELSIUS:
SCALING THE HEIGHTS OF SCIENTIFIC TEMPERATURE
1701–1744

Anders Celsius was a clever person who lived in Sweden and loved playing with temperatures and inventing cool ways to measure heat and cold.

Anders invented the Celsius temperature scale, which we often use today. On the Celsius scale, the freezing point of water is zero degrees, and the boiling point is one hundred degrees. It's a simple way to measure how hot or cold something is.

But Anders didn't stop there! He also came up with the idea of dividing the circle into 360 degrees, which we now use for angles and navigation. So, he wasn't just a temperature guy; he was a math whiz too! Anders loved learning and teaching others about science and math. He was a professor at a university in Sweden, where he shared his knowledge with students and inspired them to explore the wonders of the world.

Anders' Celsius scale is still used by scientists, meteorologists, and everyday people all over the world. Thanks to him, we can easily talk about how hot or cold it is outside!

How can you challenge yourself to measure and record temperatures in your environment over time to observe changes?

°C
100°
0°
Anders Celsius
1701 - 1744
Sweden
Mathematician
Physicist
Astronomer
Centigrade Scale

FRIEDRICH MOHS:
MEASURING THE HARDNESS OF MINERALS
1773–1839

Friederich Mohs was born in Germany in 1773. As a child, he loved collecting rocks and minerals. He was so curious about them that he decided to study them when he grew up.

One day, Friederich had a big idea: what if he could create a special scale to measure how hard or soft different minerals were? He wanted to know which minerals were the toughest and which ones were the easiest to scratch.

So, Friederich started testing different minerals. He scratched one mineral with another to see which one left a mark. If a mineral would scratch another, it was harder. If it got scratched, it was softer. He tested a lot of minerals this way and finally came up with a list of ten minerals, each one harder than the one before it.

He called this list the Mohs Scale of Hardness. On his scale, he put talc, the softest mineral, at number one. Talc is so soft you can scratch it with your fingernail! At the other end, at number ten, he put diamond, the hardest mineral of all. Diamonds are so tough that they can scratch any other mineral!

Here's a fun fact: you can even test some minerals yourself with Friederich's scale. For example, if you have a piece of glass (which is about 5.5 on the Mohs scale), you can see if it gets scratched by a knife blade (which is harder) or if it scratches a piece of chalk (which is softer). Just be sure to ask for permission before you scratch objects in your home or school!

Friederich's scale helps scientists, jewelers, and even kids like you understand how tough different minerals are.

Have you ever tried to scratch or break different rocks or minerals to see which one is the hardest?

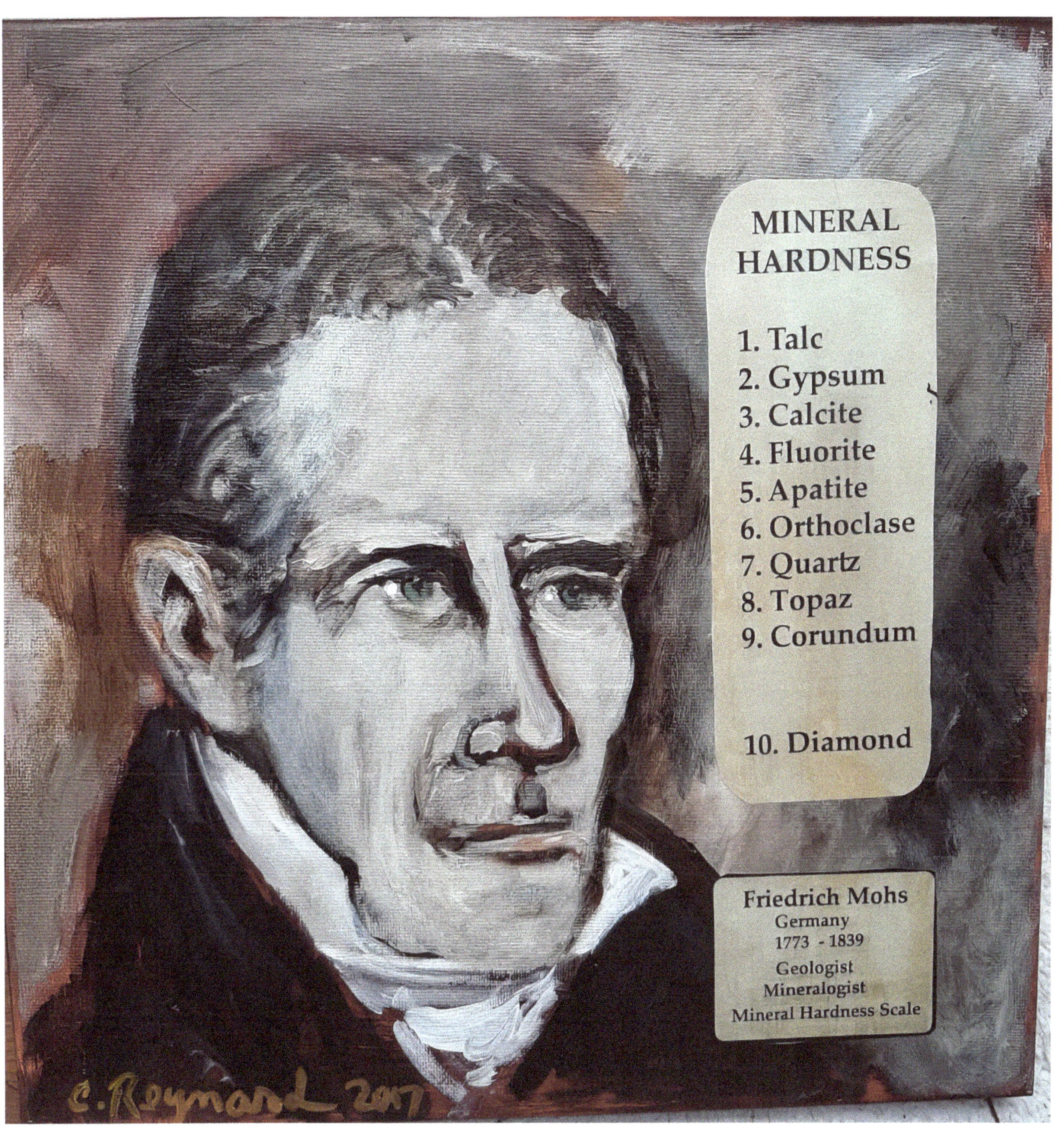

MINERAL HARDNESS

1. Talc
2. Gypsum
3. Calcite
4. Fluorite
5. Apatite
6. Orthoclase
7. Quartz
8. Topaz
9. Corundum

10. Diamond

Friedrich Mohs
Germany
1773 - 1839
Geologist
Mineralogist
Mineral Hardness Scale

JOHANNES GEIGER:
COUNTING COSMIC RAYS ACROSS THE UNIVERSE
1882–1945

Johannes Geiger, also known as Hans, was a smart scientist who was born and lived in Germany. He loved to think about and observe the effects of tiny, invisible things.

Hans is famous for inventing a special tool called the Geiger counter. This device helps scientists detect and measure radioactivity, which is a type of energy some materials give off. Radioactivity is like invisible rays or tiny particles flying around, and the Geiger counter can sense them.

Here's how it works: when radioactive particles hit the Geiger counter, it makes a clicking sound or shows a reading on a dial. The more clicks or higher the reading, the more radiation there is. It's like having a super-sensitive ear that can hear tiny whispers that no one else can hear!

Geiger used his invention to help other scientists understand more about radioactivity and atomic particles. His work was key for studying how atoms work, and it has even helped in medicine and keeping people safe from high radiation.

Hans Geiger was a detective of the invisible, creating a cool gadget to help us understand things we can't see with our eyes. His Geiger counter helps keep us safe and learn more about the tiny particles that make up our world!

Have you ever wondered how scientists like Hans Geiger use instruments to explore the invisible world around us? What would you like to discover using similar tools?

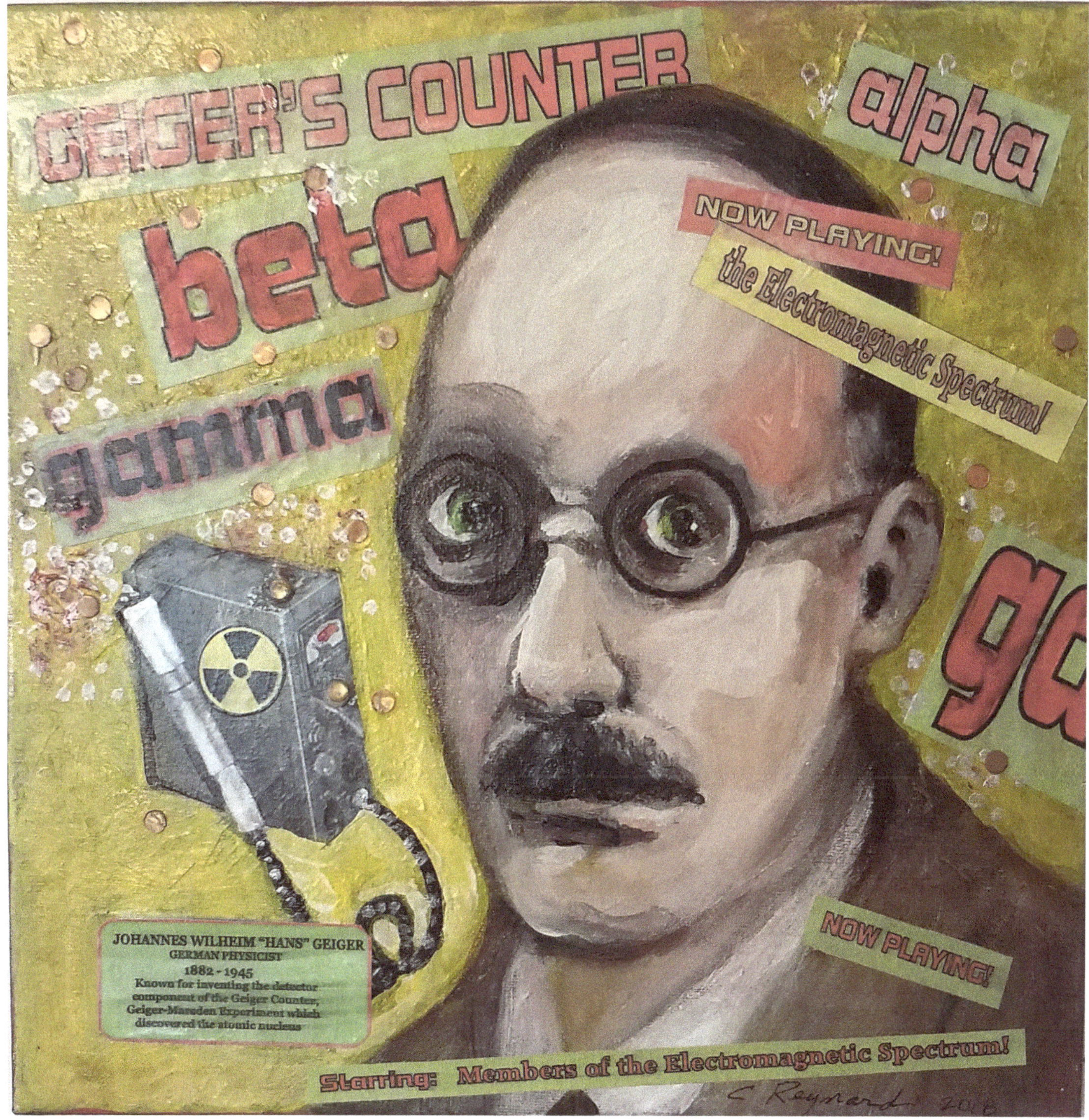

GEIGER'S COUNTER
alpha
NOW PLAYING!
the Electromagnetic Spectrum!
beta
gamma
ga
JOHANNES WILHELM "HANS" GEIGER
GERMAN PHYSICIST
1882 - 1945
Known for inventing the detector
component of the Geiger Counter,
Geiger-Marsden Experiment which
discovered the atomic nucleus
NOW PLAYING!
Starring: Members of the Electromagnetic Spectrum!
C Reynards 2018

CHAPTER 5

DEVELOPERS OF SCIENTIFIC LAWS

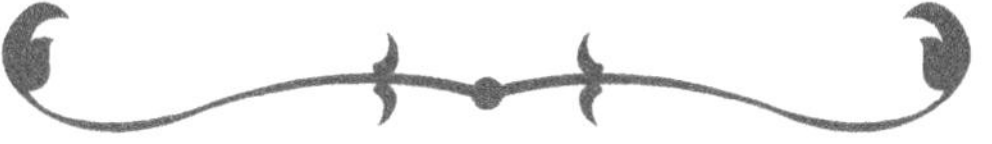

Sir Isaac Newton:
Mastering the Laws of Motion and Gravity
1643–1727

Sir Isaac Newton was a brilliant thinker who was born and lived in England. He loved to ask questions and figure out how things worked.

One day, when Isaac was sitting under a tree, an apple fell on his head. Instead of just brushing it off, he started thinking about why the apple fell instead of floating away. This led him to come up with the idea of gravity, which is the force that pulls things toward the ground.

Isaac also discovered something called Newton's Laws of Motion. These laws explain how objects move when forces act on them. For example, his first law says that an object will keep doing what it's doing unless a force makes it change. So, if you roll a ball on the ground, it will keep rolling until a force, such as gravity, friction, or your foot, stops it!

His discoveries were so important that they changed how people thought about the world. He even made a super cool telescope to look at the stars and discover new things about the universe.

Isaac Newton was a superhero of science, using his brain to solve mysteries and explain how the world works. He showed us that even the simplest observations, like apples falling from trees, can lead to big discoveries when we ask, "Why?"

What's something you've always wondered about, like Newton wondered about gravity?

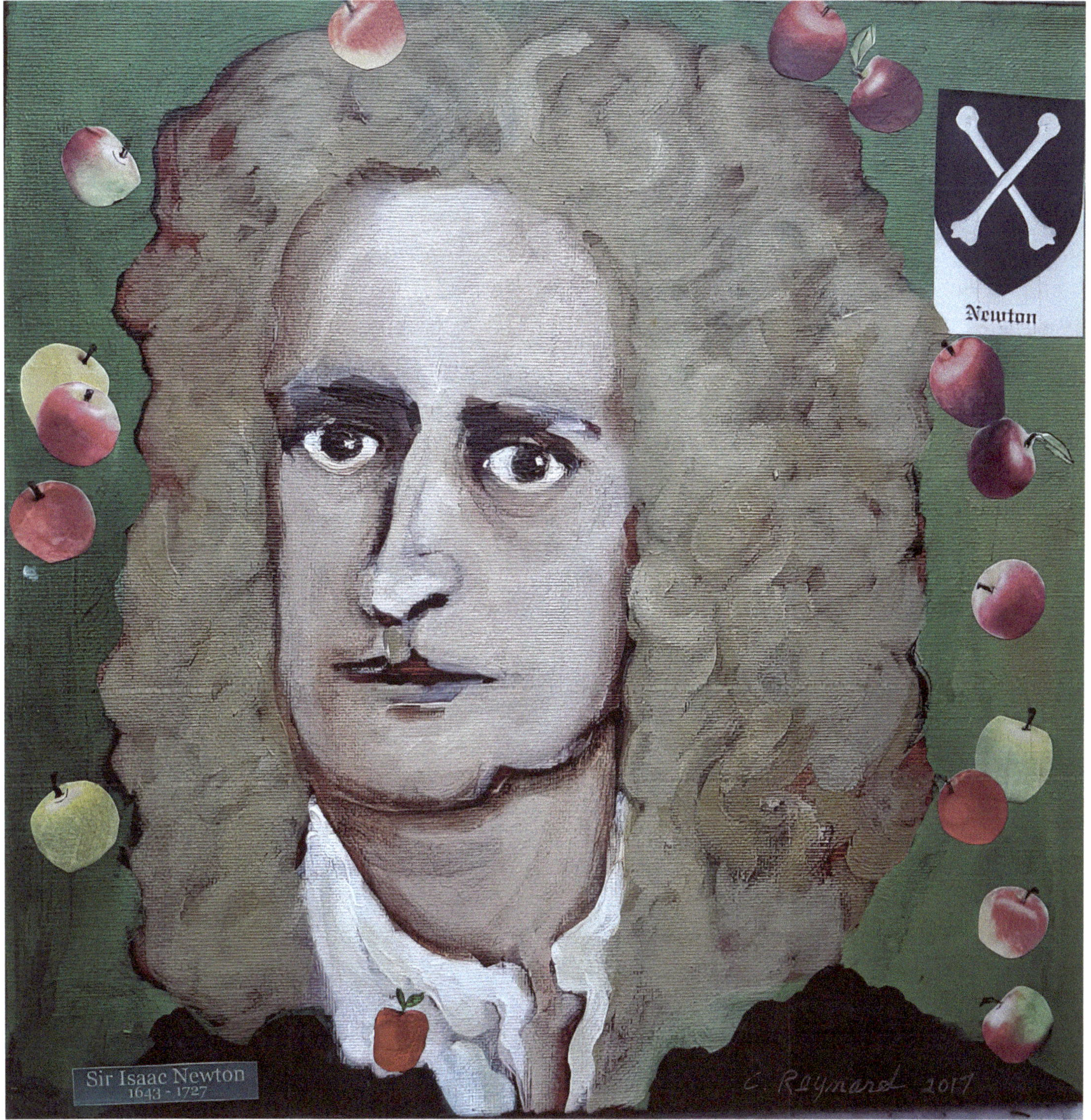

Newton
Sir Isaac Newton
1643 - 1727
C. Reymard 2017

SIR GEORGE STOKES:
MASTERING THE MAGIC OF RAINBOWS
1819–1903

Sir George Stokes was born in 1819 in Ireland. He was really smart and always wanted to learn more about the world.

As a child, George liked to watch the water in streams and rivers. He wondered why it flowed the way it did and why some objects floated while others sank. His curiosity about water and how it moved would later become very important in his work as a scientist.

When George grew up, he became a physicist, which means he studied how things move and interact with each other. One of his big discoveries was about something called fluid dynamics. That's a fancy way of saying he figured out how fluids like water and air move and behave.

George Stokes studied how waves move in water and even how tiny particles move through liquids. He wrote down his ideas in books and papers so that other scientists could learn from him too. He also studied how light bends and changes when it moves through different materials, which helped us understand how rainbows form!

George Stokes was so good at what he did that he became a professor at a university, where he taught many students about physics and how to study things scientifically.

Scientists still use Sir George Stoke's ideas to understand how fluids move, which helps us improve the design of things like boats and airplanes.

Sir George Stokes studied how fluids move. Have you ever noticed how liquids like water and syrup move differently and wondered why?

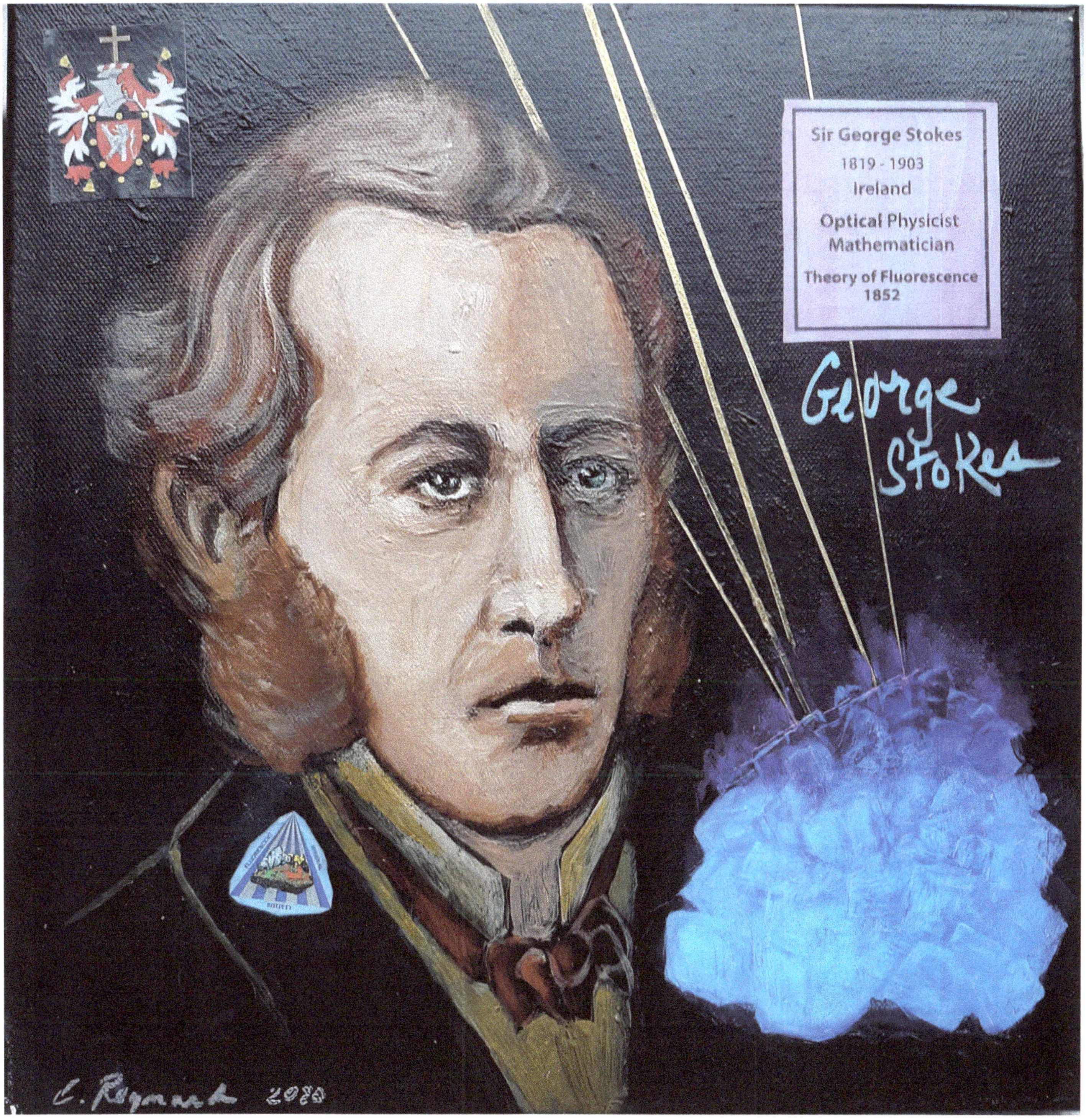

Sir George Stokes
1819 - 1903
Ireland
Optical Physicist
Mathematician
Theory of Fluorescence
1852
George Stokes
C. Reymann 2020

ALBERT EINSTEIN:
LEARNING THE SECRET DANCE OF TIME AND SPACE
1879–1955

Born in Germany in 1879, Albert Einstein was a brilliant man with a wild head of white hair who loved to think about the world in unusual ways. He always asked, "Why?" and "How?" about everything around him. But he didn't just ask questions; he tried to find the answers, even when they were very tricky.

One of his most famous ideas is called relativity. This is a way of understanding how time and space work together, like a big cosmic dance. It's a bit like imagining that time can stretch and shrink, and space can bend and twist. Arthur Eddington, a famous astronomer and physicist who you will hear about later in this book, did experiments that supported Einstein's theory of relativity and helped other scientists understand how the universe works.

Einstein loved to play the violin, and he thought music was like a special kind of math that you could hear with your ears. He also had a great sense of humor and liked to laugh and have fun, even while thinking about serious science stuff.

In short, Albert Einstein was a genius who looked at the world with wonder, just like a curious child. He helped us see the universe in a whole new way!

Albert Einstein had big ideas about space, time, and energy. What's an idea you have that could change the way we understand the world?

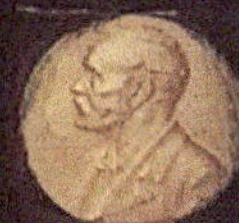

E = mc²
BIG BANG MONTHLY
bigbangsci.com   fall issue 2020
ALBERT EINSTEIN
1879 - 1955
German
Theoritical Physicist
Theory of Relativity

CHAPTER 6

EXPLORERS OF THE QUANTUM FRONTIER

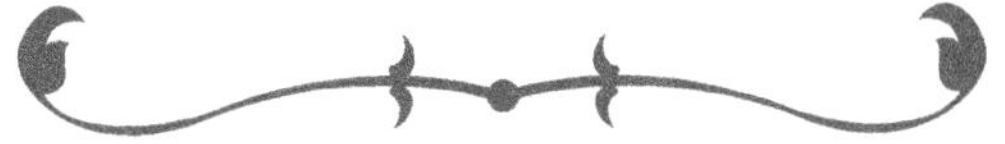

ERNEST RUTHERFORD:
SPLITTING ATOMS, UNVEILING SECRETS
1871–1937

Ernest Rutherford was a super curious scientist who was born in Brightwater, New Zealand and loved to explore the tiniest building blocks of everything around us. Imagine someone who's always asking, "What's inside that?" and "How does it work?" about everything they see. That was Ernest!

Rutherford liked to study tiny particles called atoms, which are like the building blocks of everything in the world.

One of his most famous experiments was when he shot tiny particles called alpha particles at gold foil. He expected the alpha particles to go straight through the foil, but some bounced back! This was a big surprise and led him to discover that atoms are mostly empty space, with a small, dense nucleus in the middle. The nucleus is surrounded by particles called electrons.

Rutherford's discoveries helped us understand how atoms are put together and how they behave. His work laid the foundation for modern physics and our understanding of the universe.

Even though his ideas might seem tricky, Rutherford had a fun and curious spirit that made science exciting for everyone. He showed us that even the smallest things can hold big surprises!

What tiny things would you like to explore and understand better, like atoms and their parts?

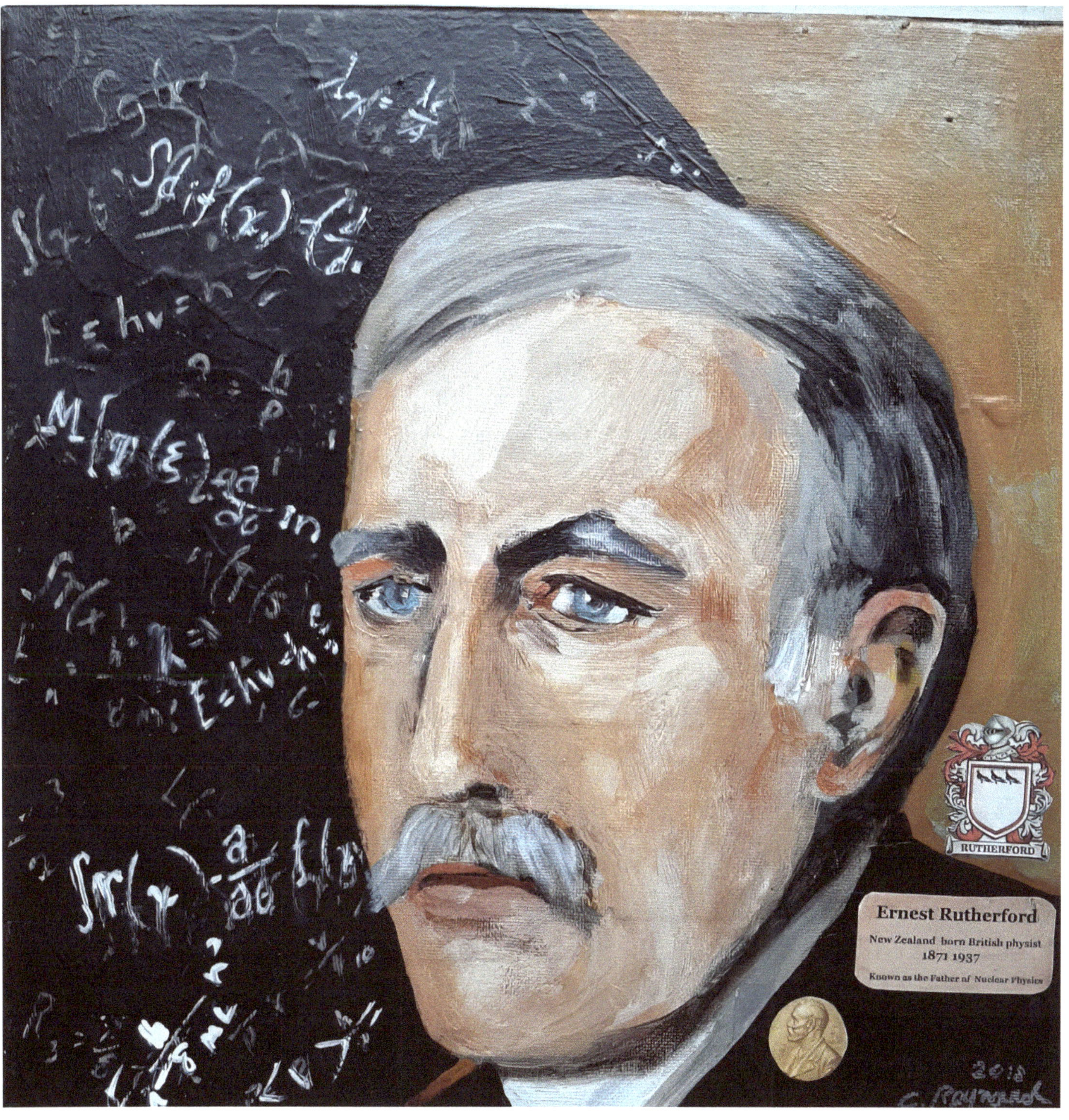

RUTHERFORD
Ernest Rutherford
New Zealand born British physist
1871 1937
Known as the Father of Nuclear Physics

MARIE CURIE:
RADIANT DISCOVERIES
1867–1934

Marie Curie was born in Warsaw, Poland but spent much of her grownup life in France. Both of her parents were teachers of physics and mathematics. Marie's father's scientific tools fascinated Marie! Her parents encouraged Marie to observe and wonder about the world around her.

Marie was very interested in tiny, invisible things called atoms that make up everything around us. She discovered two special elements, which are types of atoms, and named them polonium and radium. These elements were very different from the ones scientists had known because they could give off energy, which we now call radioactivity.

Marie didn't just make these discoveries; she also did a lot of experiments to understand how radioactivity worked. She was the first woman to win a Nobel Prize, which is a big award for people who make an important discovery or change in the world. In fact, she won it twice!

Marie worked hard and was very brave, especially because it wasn't easy for women to be scientists back then. She showed everyone that girls can be just as good at science as boys.

Marie Curie's discoveries help us today in many ways. One of the ways is in medicine where radiation is used to treat sick people. She was a true science hero who loved learning and discovering new things, and she inspired many people to follow their dreams and explore the wonders of science!

How does Marie Curie's dedication to science encourage you to explore your own interests?

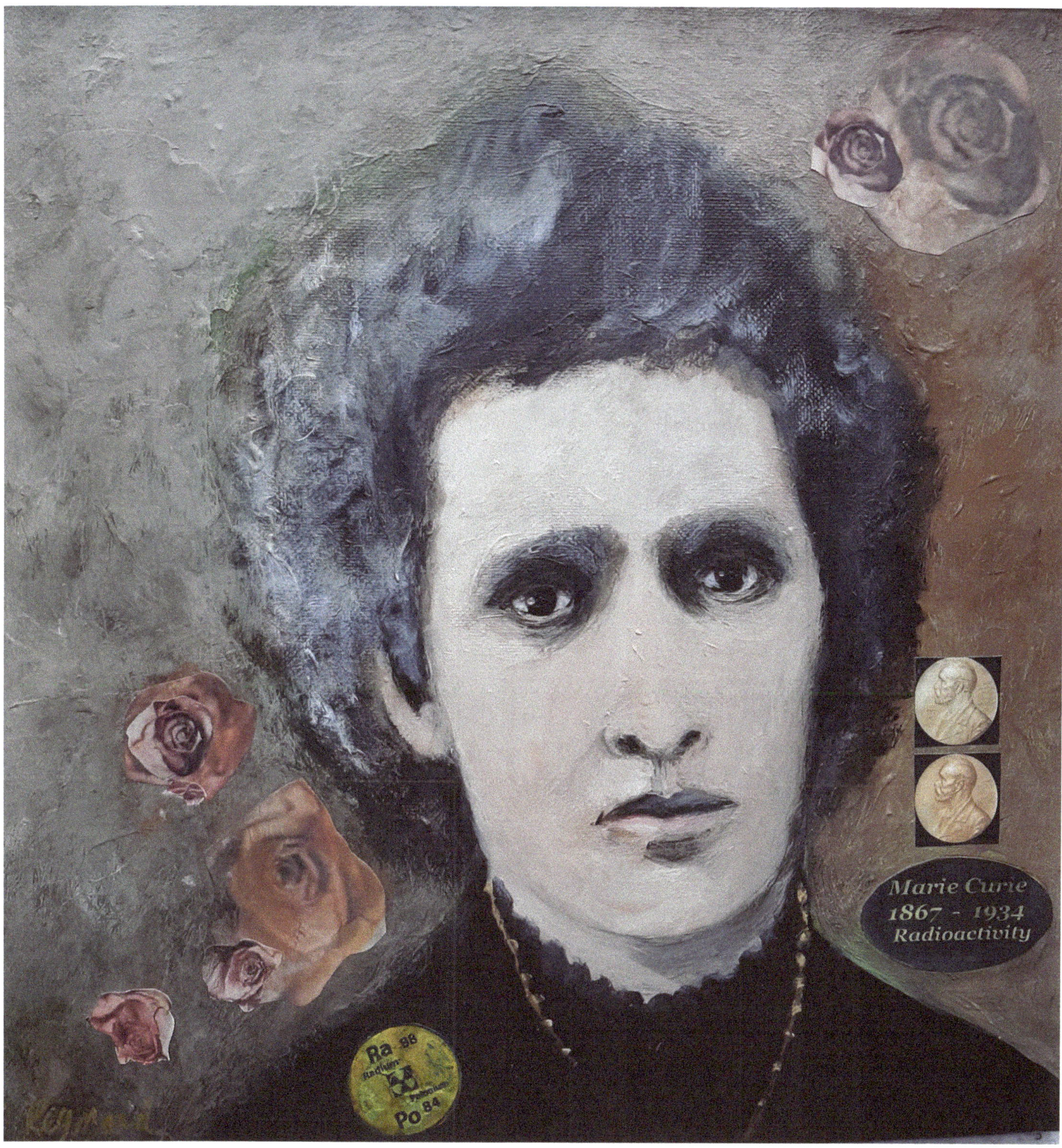
Ra 88
Radium
Polonium
Po 84
Marie Curie
1867 - 1934
Radioactivity

ENRICO FERMI: UNLOCKING ATOMIC POWER
1901–1954

Enrico Fermi was born in 1901 in Italy. Enrico was a curious boy who loved to ask questions about everything around him. He would spend hours tinkering with gadgets and toys, trying to understand how they worked.

As a child, Enrico was especially fascinated by mathematics and physics. He loved solving puzzles and figuring out how things moved and interacted. His parents saw how smart he was and encouraged him to learn more about science.

When Enrico grew up, he became a physicist. He studied the smallest particles that make up everything in the universe. One of Enrico Fermi's biggest discoveries was about atoms and how they release energy. He figured out how to make atoms split apart in a controlled way, which is called nuclear fission.

During World War II, Enrico Fermi moved to the United States because of the war in Europe. There, he worked on a secret project called the Manhattan Project. This project was about building the first atomic bomb, a powerful weapon that could change the course of the war.

After the war, Enrico Fermi continued to study atoms and particles. He made many important contributions to our understanding of how the universe works at the tiniest levels. He won a Nobel Prize in Physics for his work on nuclear reactions and discovering new particles.

Enrico Fermi loved teaching and sharing his knowledge with students. He believed in asking questions and exploring new ideas, which inspired many young scientists to follow in his footsteps.

Scientists today still study nuclear reactions and use Enrico's ideas to create new technologies and understand the universe better. Enrico Fermi showed us that by being curious and asking questions, we can unlock incredible secrets about the world around us!

Enrico Fermi studied atoms and nuclear reactions. What's something small that you've seen in science class or at home that you think is really interesting?

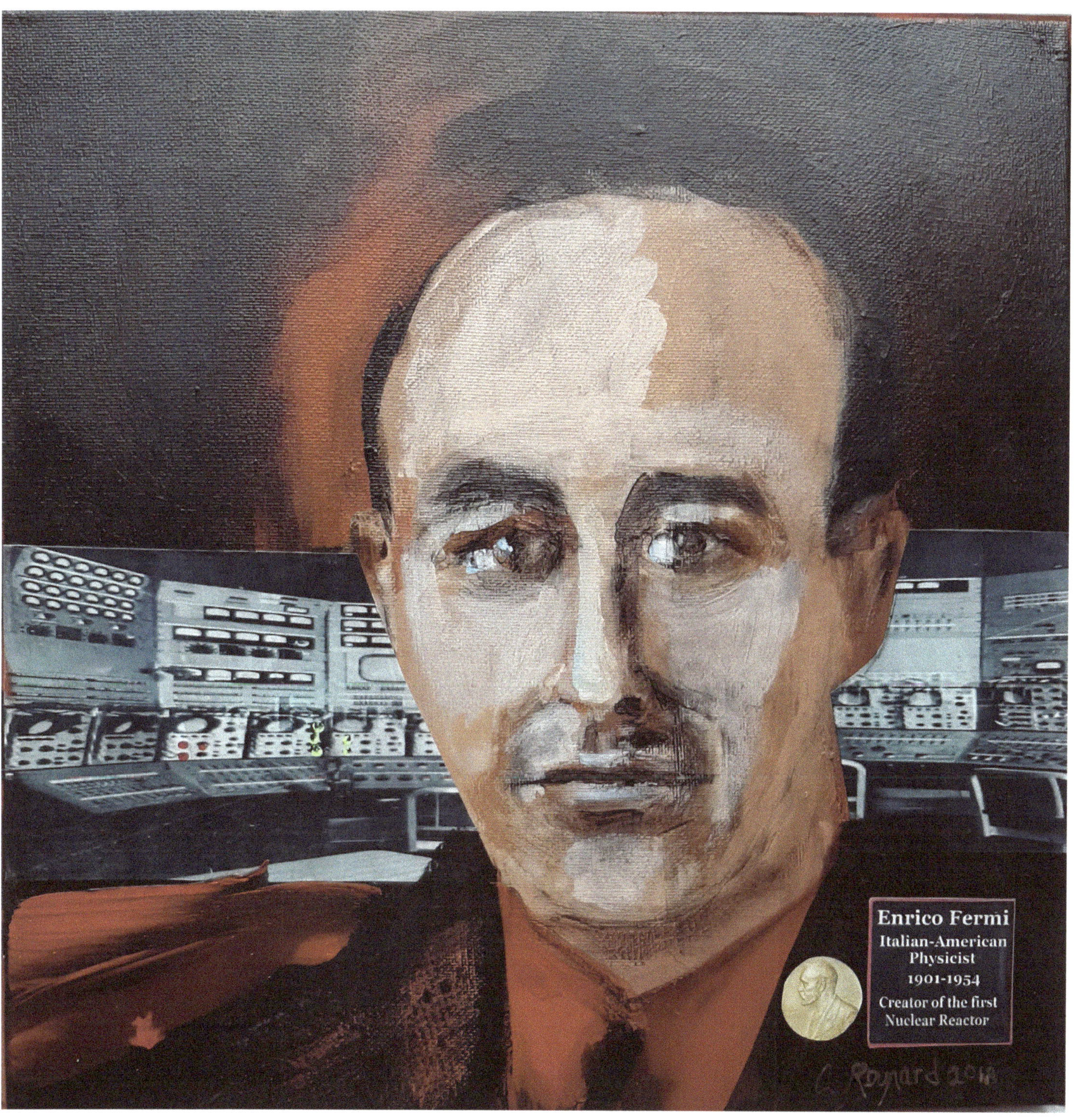

Enrico Fermi
Italian-American
Physicist
1901-1954
Creator of the first
Nuclear Reactor
C. Ronard 2018

ERWIN SCHRÖDINGER:
QUANTUM LEAPS INTO THE UNKNOWN
1887–1961

Erwin Schrödinger was a scientist who lived not so long ago, in the 1900s. He was born in Austria and loved thinking about tiny things like atoms and molecules.

One of his big discoveries was something called the Schrödinger equation. It helps us understand how tiny particles, like electrons, move around inside atoms. This was a big deal because it helped scientists learn more about the building blocks of everything in the universe!

Later, Schrödinger shared the Nobel Prize in Physics in 1933 with another scientist named Paul Dirac. They won the prize for their work on new theories about atoms and how they work.

In 1935, Schrödinger's cat became famous because he used it to help fellow scientists understand how tiny things work. Schrodinger used his cat to illustrate how some of his fellow scientists were misinterpreting quantum theory.

Erwin Schrödinger's ideas are still really important in science today. He showed us new ways to think about the tiniest parts of everything around us, and that's why people remember him as a great scientist!

Erwin Schrödinger developed ideas about quantum mechanics and shared them with others using his cat. How can you use objects to help explain your ideas when others don't understand?

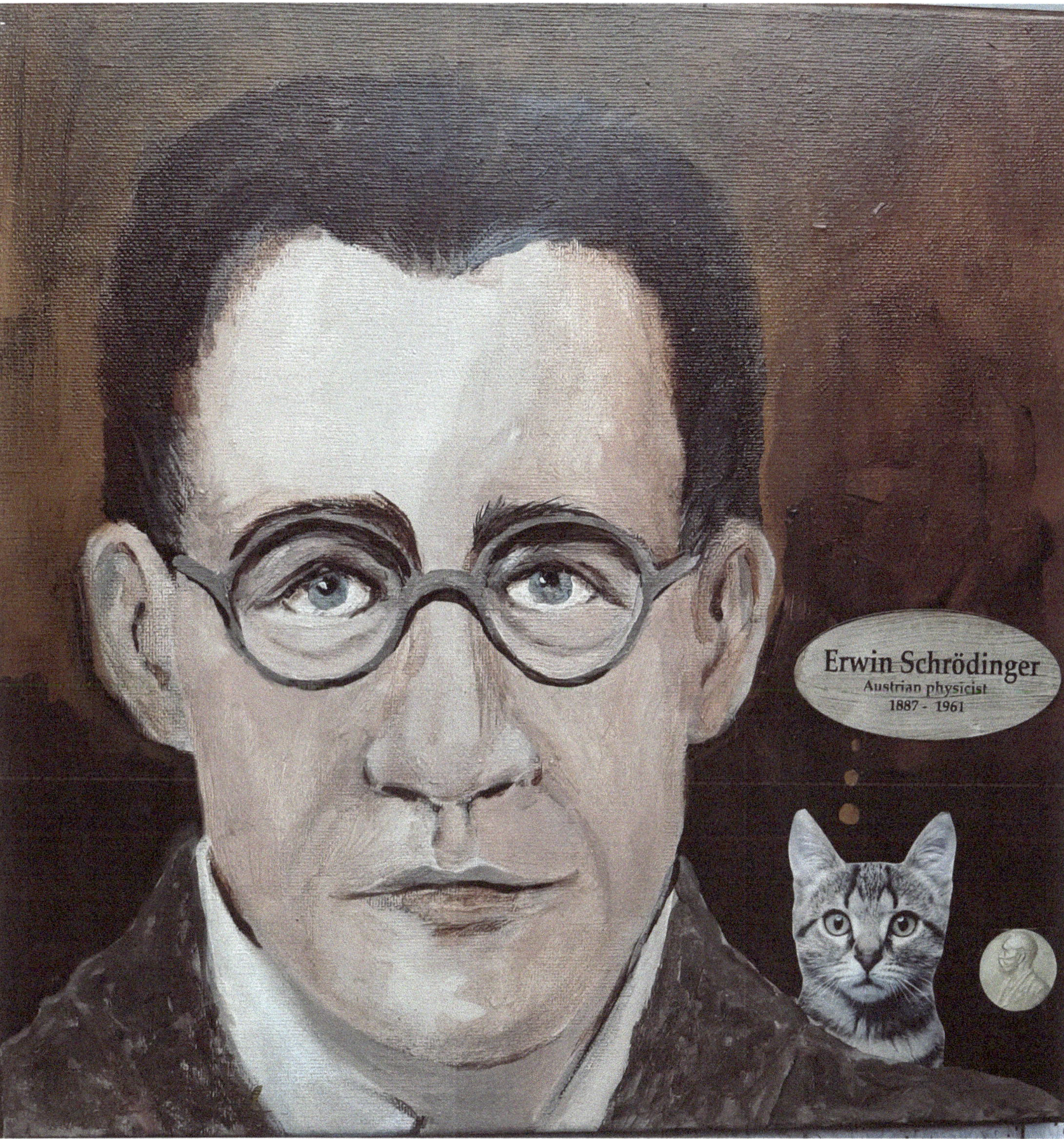

Erwin Schrödinger
Austrian physicist
1887 - 1961

JAMES CHADWICK:
DISCOVERING THE NEUTRON
1891–1974

James Chadwick was a scientist who lived in the 1900s. He was from England and loved figuring out how tiny things in the universe worked.

One of his biggest discoveries was a part of an atom he called the neutron. James knew from previous research, especially from Ernest Rutherford's work, that a tiny particle called an alpha particle could be used to investigate the structure of atoms. Chadwick placed a thin film of a light element, like beryllium, in the path of alpha particles. When alpha particles hit the beryllium, they knocked particles out of the beryllium atoms. These particles had a similar mass to the part of the atom we call protons. Protons have a positive electric charge, but these newly discovered particles had no electric charge, so James thought of them as neutral and named them neutrons.

Chadwick realized that he had discovered a new particle that no one had observed: the neutron. This discovery was super important because it helped scientists understand more about atoms and how they stick together.

Because of his discovery, James Chadwick won the Nobel Prize in Physics in 1935. Chadwick's work with neutrons paved the way for important advancements in nuclear physics, including the development of nuclear energy and applications in medicine. His discovery continues to play a vital role in scientific research and technology today. What's something you've discovered in science class or at home that made you excited to learn more?

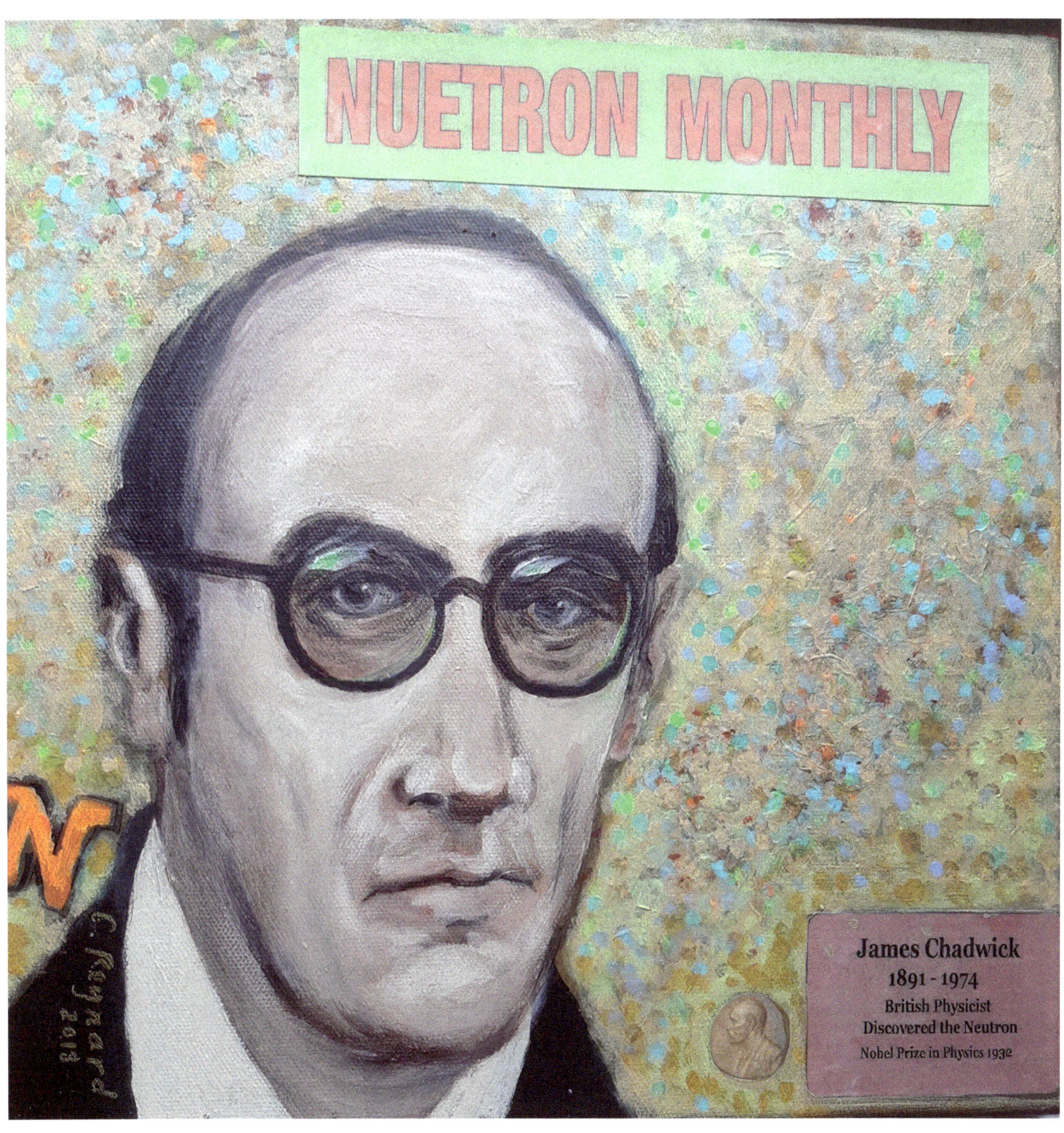

NUETRON MONTHLY
James Chadwick
1891 - 1974
British Physicist
Discovered the Neutron
Nobel Prize in Physics 1932

NIKOLA TESLA: HARNESSING LIGHTNING FOR A NEW AGE
1856–1943

Nikola Tesla was like a real-life wizard who made incredible things happen with electricity! He was born in 1856, in a country called Croatia. As a child, he loved to read and think up all sorts of inventions in his mind. As he grew older, he wanted to make his ideas come to life, so he studied hard and became an inventor.

One of Tesla's coolest inventions was the alternating current (AC) system. This is the way electricity travels through power lines to our homes so we can have lights, TV, and all the other things that need electricity. Before Tesla, people used a different kind of electricity that wasn't as good for traveling long distances. Tesla's AC system changed the world by making it possible to send electricity over very long distances so everyone could use it.

Tesla also loved to do experiments. He even made a machine called the Tesla coil, which could create huge sparks of electricity that looked like lightning. It was like he had the power of a thunderstorm in his lab!

Even though some of his ideas seemed like magic, they were based on science and helped create many of the technologies we use today. Tesla's work laid the foundation for things like radio, wireless communication, and even the development of modern robots.

Nikola Tesla was like a genius inventor who dreamed up amazing things and made them real. He showed us that with imagination, hard work, and scientific knowledge, we can create incredible inventions that change the world.

Nikola Tesla was a genius inventor who imagined and created amazing new technologies. What inventions or ideas do you dream of creating that could make life better or more fun for people around the world?

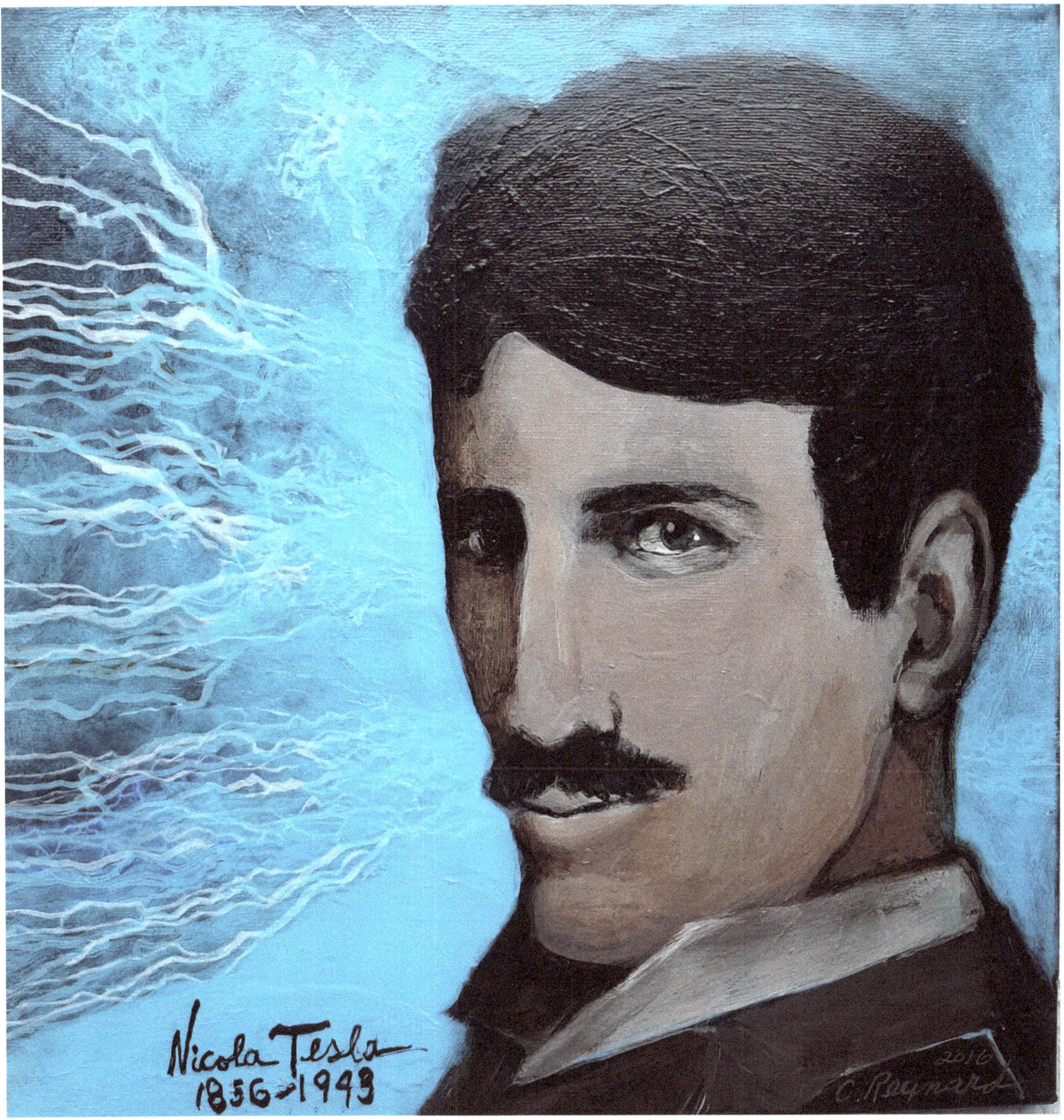

Nicola Tesla
1856-1943

MAX PLANCK:
THE QUANTUM QUEST
1858–1947

Long ago, there was a scientist named Max Planck. He was born in 1858 in Germany. Max was a curious boy who loved to explore the world around him. He would spend hours in his backyard, watching insects and birds and wondering how everything worked. When Max grew up, he became a physicist and studied the smallest particles that make up everything in the universe.

Max Planck figured out that light and energy behave in ways that are different from what scientists had thought before. He showed that energy is not continuous and can only be released or absorbed in specific amounts. This discovery laid the foundation for a whole new branch of physics called quantum theory.

Max Planck's ideas were so important that they changed how scientists understood atoms, molecules, and how the universe works at its most basic level. His work led to many other discoveries in physics and helped create new technologies that we use today.

Max's discoveries are still really important in physics today. Scientists still use quantum theory to study everything from computers to space exploration. Max Planck showed us that by being curious and asking questions, we can uncover amazing secrets.

Max Planck studied how energy works in atoms. What's something you've learned about energy that you think is really cool?

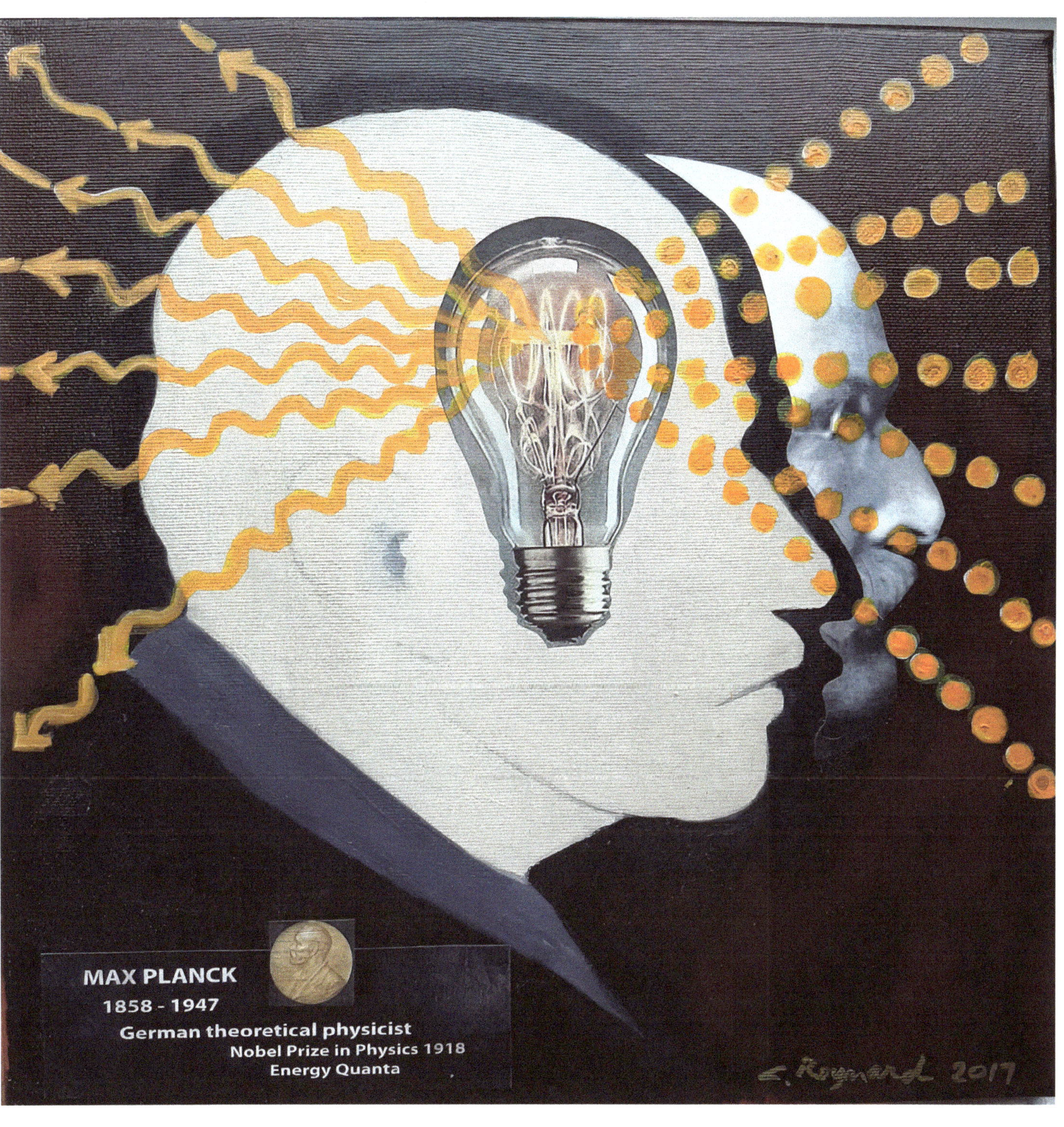

MAX PLANCK
1858 - 1947
German theoretical physicist
Nobel Prize in Physics 1918
Energy Quanta

NIELS BOHR: UNRAVELING THE QUANTUM CODE
1885–1962

Niels Bohr was born in 1885 in Denmark. When he was young, he was very curious and loved solving puzzles. He was really good at math and science, which helped him understand how things worked. As he grew older, Niels became fascinated with atoms. Atoms are the tiny building blocks that make up everything in the world, like your toys, your food, and even you! Niels wanted to understand how these tiny atoms behaved and why they did what they did.

Niels made a big discovery about atoms. He figured out that atoms have a center, called a nucleus, and tiny particles called electrons that zoom around the nucleus like planets around the sun. This was a brand-new way of thinking about atoms, and it helped other scientists understand how the world works.

Niels also thought a lot about how light and atoms interact. He found that when atoms absorb or give off light, they do it in tiny packets called quanta. This idea was really important and, along with the work of Max Planck and others, helped create a whole new field of science called quantum mechanics. He also won a Nobel Prize for his amazing discoveries. Because of Niels, we understand so much more about how the tiny parts of our world work. His discoveries helped pave the way for new inventions and technologies, like computers and medical equipment.

Thanks to Niels Bohr, we know a lot more about the tiny building blocks that make up everything around us. If you ever think about how things are made or see amazing technology, remember Niels and his incredible journey into the world of atoms!

Niels Bohr discovered how atoms are structured. What's something small you've discovered that helped you understand a bigger picture?

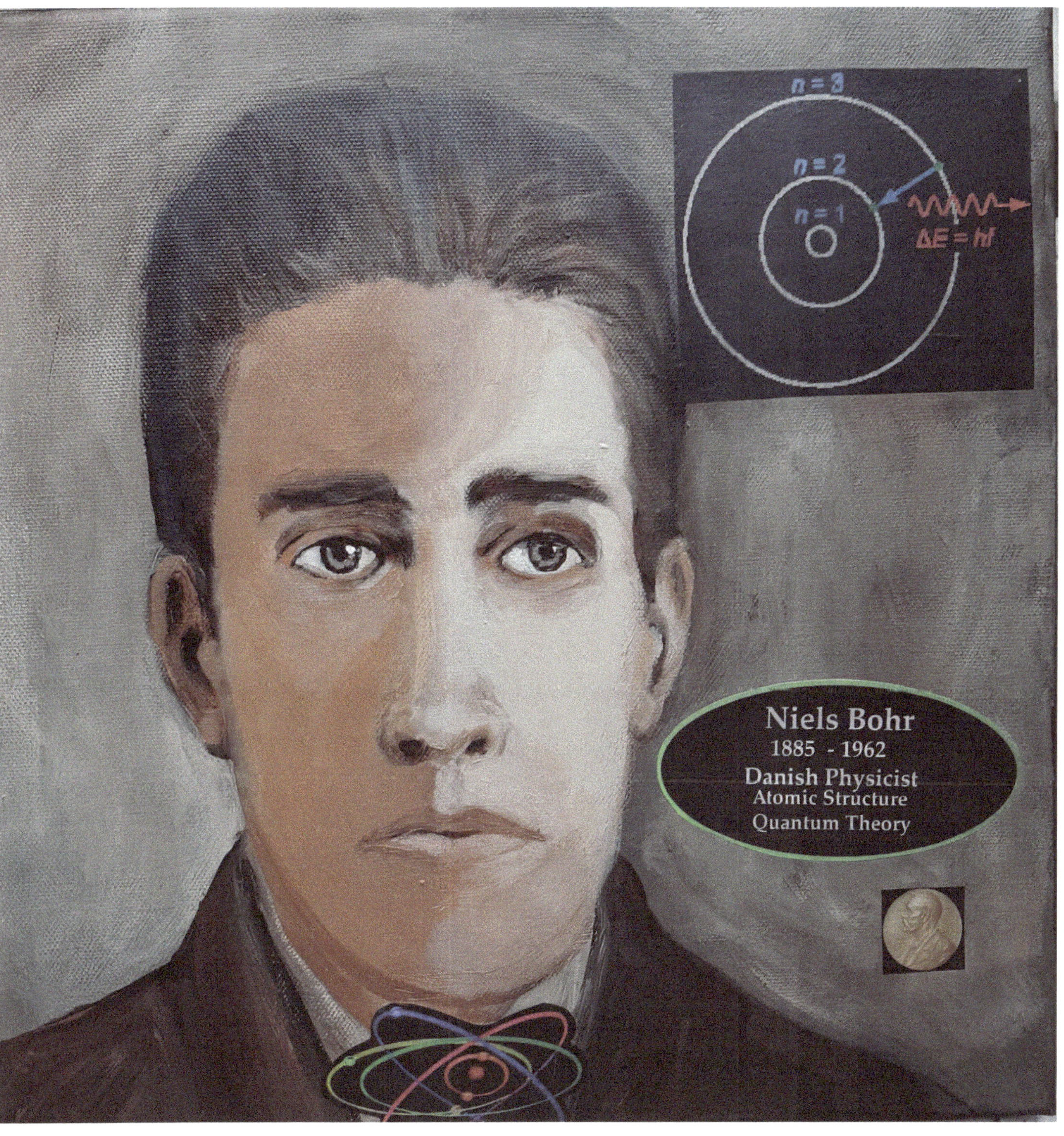

n = 3
n = 2
n = 1
ΔE = hf
Niels Bohr
1885 - 1962
Danish Physicist
Atomic Structure
Quantum Theory

CHAPTER 7

STARGAZERS EXPLORING THE COSMIC FRONTIER

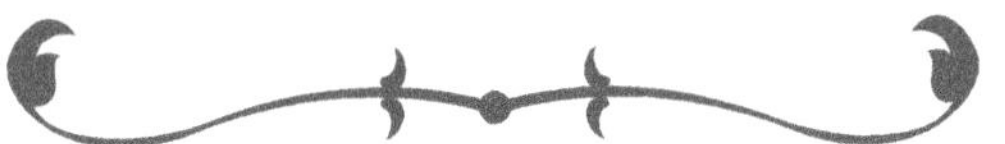

NICOLAUS COPERNICUS: REVOLUTIONIZING THE COSMIC ORDER
1473–1543

Nicolaus Copernicus was born and lived in Poland a long time ago. He loved to look at the sky and figure out how everything moved.

Copernicus had a big idea that changed the way people thought about the Earth and the planets. He believed that the Earth wasn't the center of everything like everyone thought at the time. Instead, he thought the Earth and the other planets moved around the sun.

This idea was called the heliocentric theory, and it was a big deal! Before Copernicus, people believed that everything revolved around the Earth. But Copernicus showed that the sun was actually at the center, and the Earth was just one of many planets going around it.

Even though some people didn't agree with him at first, Copernicus kept studying and learning. He wrote a book called *On the Revolutions of the Celestial Spheres*, where he explained his ideas.

Copernicus' ideas were so important because they laid the foundation for modern astronomy. They helped us and other scientists understand how the planets move and how our solar system works.

Nicolaus Copernicus was a star explorer, showing us that the Earth is just one small part of a much bigger picture and inspiring us to keep looking up at the sky and dreaming about the wonders of space!

Nicolaus Copernicus showed that the Earth orbits the Sun. How does his courage to challenge common beliefs inspire you to question and learn?

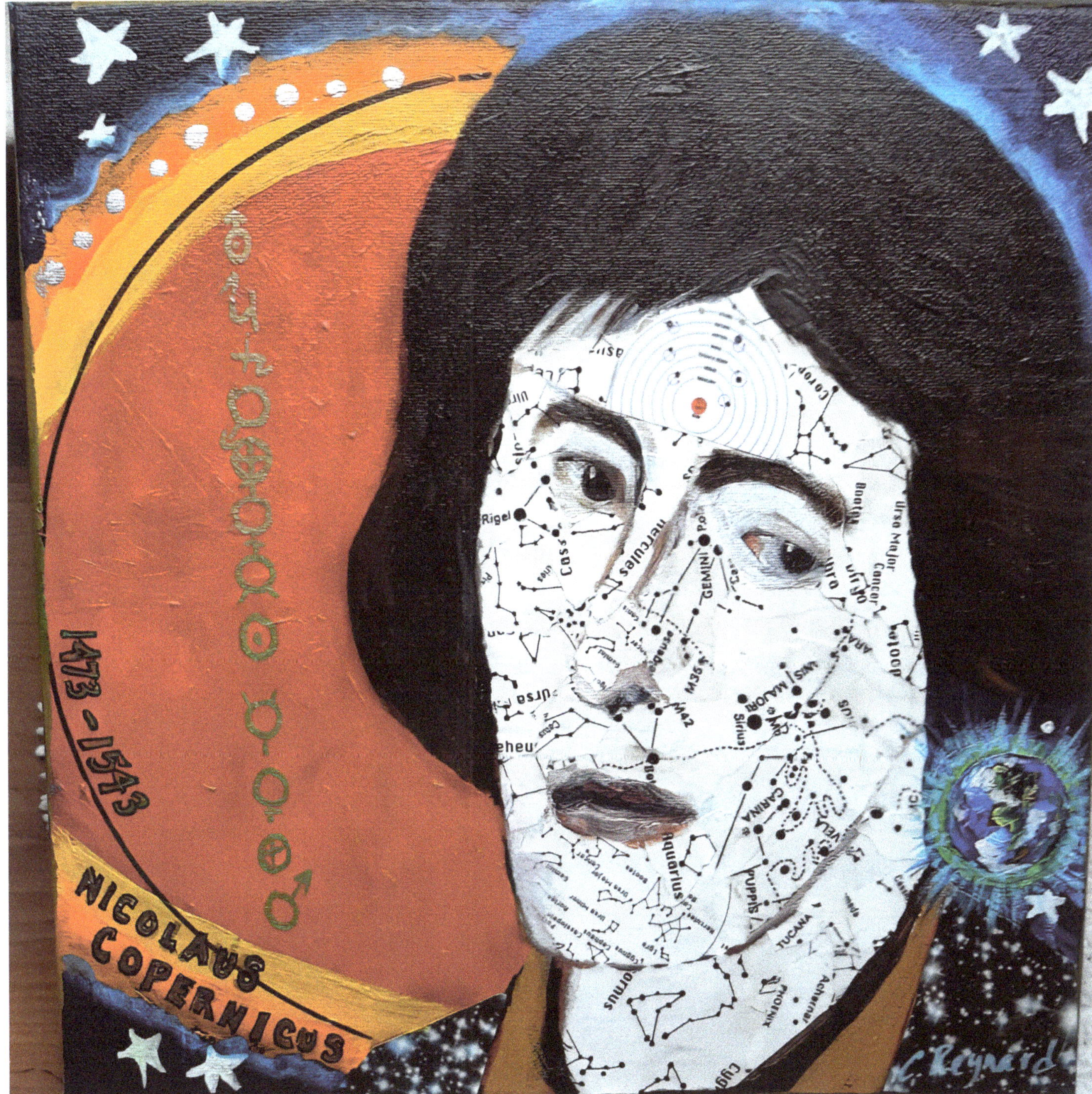

1473 - 1543
NICOLAUS COPERNICUS
Rigel
Cass
Hercules
GEMINI
Ursa Major
Cancer
Sirius
CANIS MAJORIS
CARINA
VELA
PUPPIS
Aquarius
TUCANA
PHOENIX
Achernar
Cygnus
C. Reynard

TYCHO BRAHE: DISCOVERING THE DYNAMIC UNIVERSE
1546–1606

Tycho Brahe lived in Denmark in the 1500s. Tycho was a curious child who loved looking up at the stars and wondering about the universe.

When Tycho was a boy, he saw a solar eclipse, which is when the moon covers the sun for a little while. It fascinated him and made him want to learn more about the sky and the stars. His family noticed how much he loved studying the heavens.

As Tycho grew up, he became a famous astronomer. That means he studied stars, planets, and everything in space. Tycho made really precise measurements of the stars and planets using special tools he invented. He built big instruments to help him see the sky better.

One of Tycho's biggest discoveries was about a new star in the sky. People thought the stars were fixed and never changed, but Tycho saw that this new star, which we now know was an exploding star (called a supernova), appeared suddenly and then faded away. This showed that the universe was more active than people had thought before.

Tycho also studied how planets moved around the sun. He made very accurate observations that later helped another scientist, Johannes Kepler, figure out the orbits of planets.

Tycho Brahe wrote books about his discoveries. He loved sharing what he knew with others and teaching students about the wonders of space.

Even though Tycho lived a long time ago, his work laid the foundation for modern astronomy. Scientists still learn from his careful observations and measurements. He showed us that by studying the stars and planets, we can learn amazing things about the universe we live in!

Tycho Brahe studied the stars and planets. If you could make your own observations of the night sky, what would you look for and why?

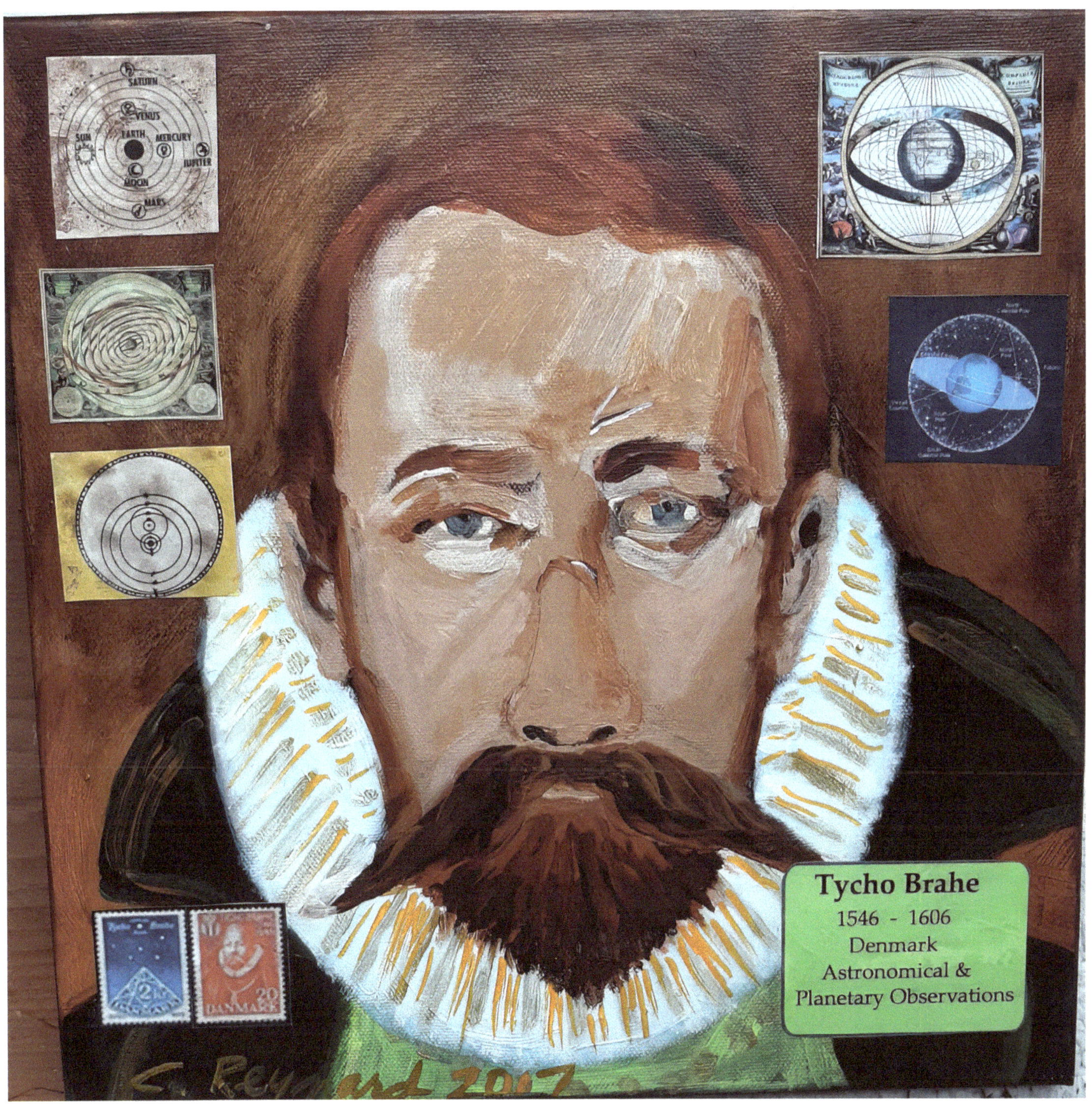

SATURN
VENUS
SUN
EARTH
MERCURY
JUPITER
MOON
MARS
DANMARK
20
Tycho Brahe
1546 - 1606
Denmark
Astronomical &
Planetary Observations
C. Reynard 2007

GALILEO:
DEFYING THE HEAVENS WITH SCIENCE
1564–1642

Galileo Galilei lived a long time ago in Italy, and he was one of the first people to use a telescope to look at the night sky. With his telescope, he made some amazing discoveries. He saw craters and mountains on the moon, spots on the sun, and even four moons orbiting around the planet Jupiter. These moons are called the Galilean moons, named after him!

Galileo was very brave because he believed that the Earth wasn't the center of the universe. Instead, he thought the Earth and other planets moved around the sun. This idea was called heliocentrism and was very different from what most people believed at the time.

He also did fun experiments to understand the effect of gravity. For example, according to a popular legend, he dropped objects of different weights from the Leaning Tower of Pisa to show that objects fall at the same speed even if their masses are different. This helped us understand gravity better.

Galileo wrote many books to share his discoveries, even though some people didn't agree with him. He showed us that it's important to ask questions, explore, experiment, and learn from what we see. If you could build your own telescope like Galileo Galilei did, what would you hope to discover about the stars and planets?

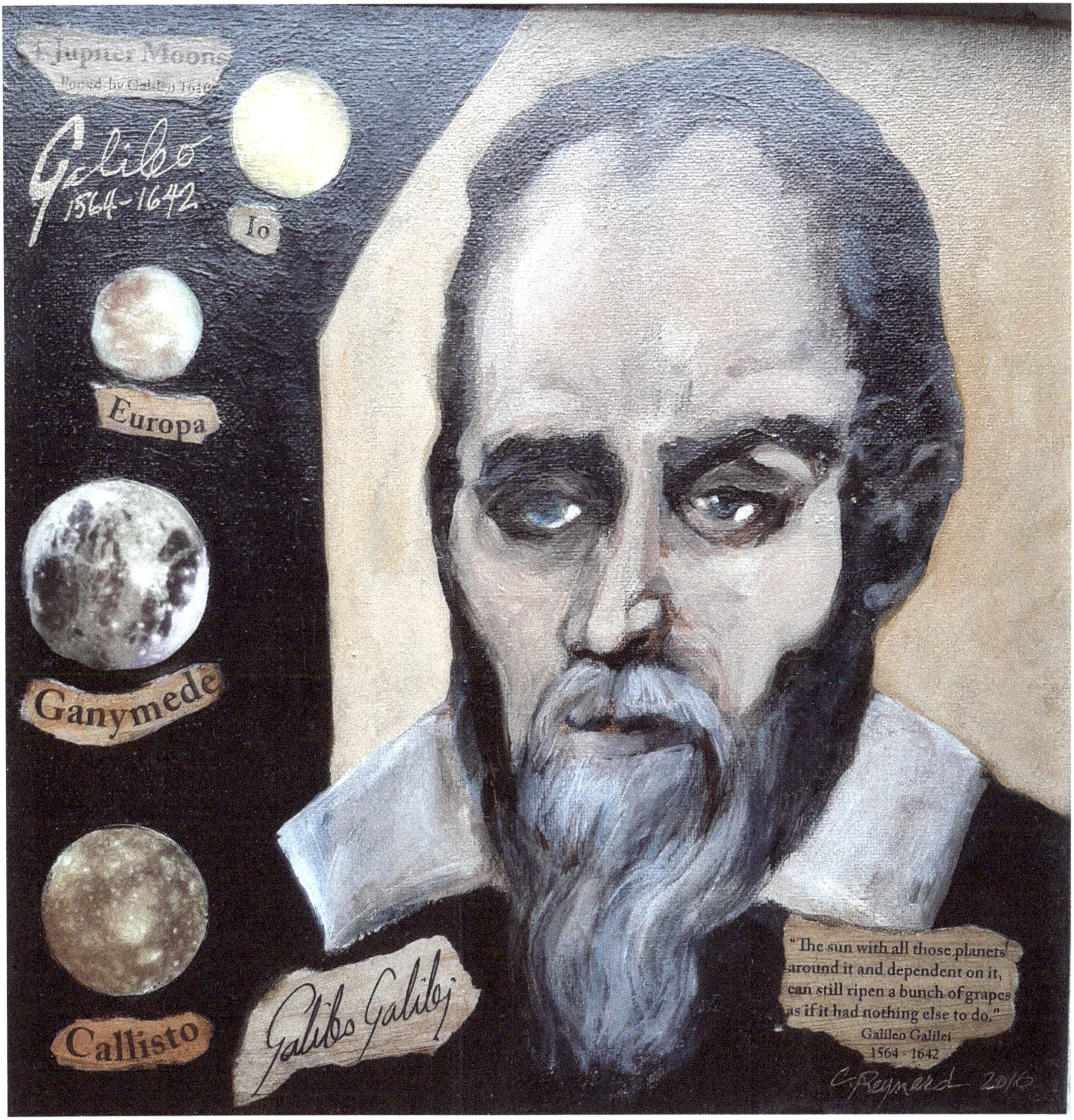

Jupiter Moons
Viewed by Galileo 1610
Galileo
1564-1642
Io
Europa
Ganymede
Callisto
Galileo Galilej
"The sun with all those planets
around it and dependent on it,
can still ripen a bunch of grapes
as if it had nothing else to do."
Galileo Galilei
1564 - 1642
C Reynard 2016

JOHANNES KEPLER:
UNLOCKING THE CELESTIAL DANCE OF PLANETS
1571–1630

Johannes Kepler was born and lived long ago in Germany, before telescopes were very good. He worked really hard to understand the way planets move around the sun. He used lots of math and very careful observations to figure things out.

He discovered something very cool: planets don't move in perfect circles around the sun. Instead, they move in shapes called ellipses, which are like stretched-out circles. This was a big surprise at the time and helped scientists understand our solar system much better.

Kepler also found that planets move faster when they are closer to the sun and slower when they are farther away. He wrote down these ideas in what we now call Kepler's laws.

Even though he lived a long time ago, Kepler's discoveries are still important today. They help us understand how rockets travel in space and how to find new planets around other stars.

Johannes Kepler was a star detective, solving the mysteries of the night sky and helping us learn more about the universe! He studied the motions of planets and discovered their orbits. What's something in nature that moves in a predictable way, like the planets Kepler studied?

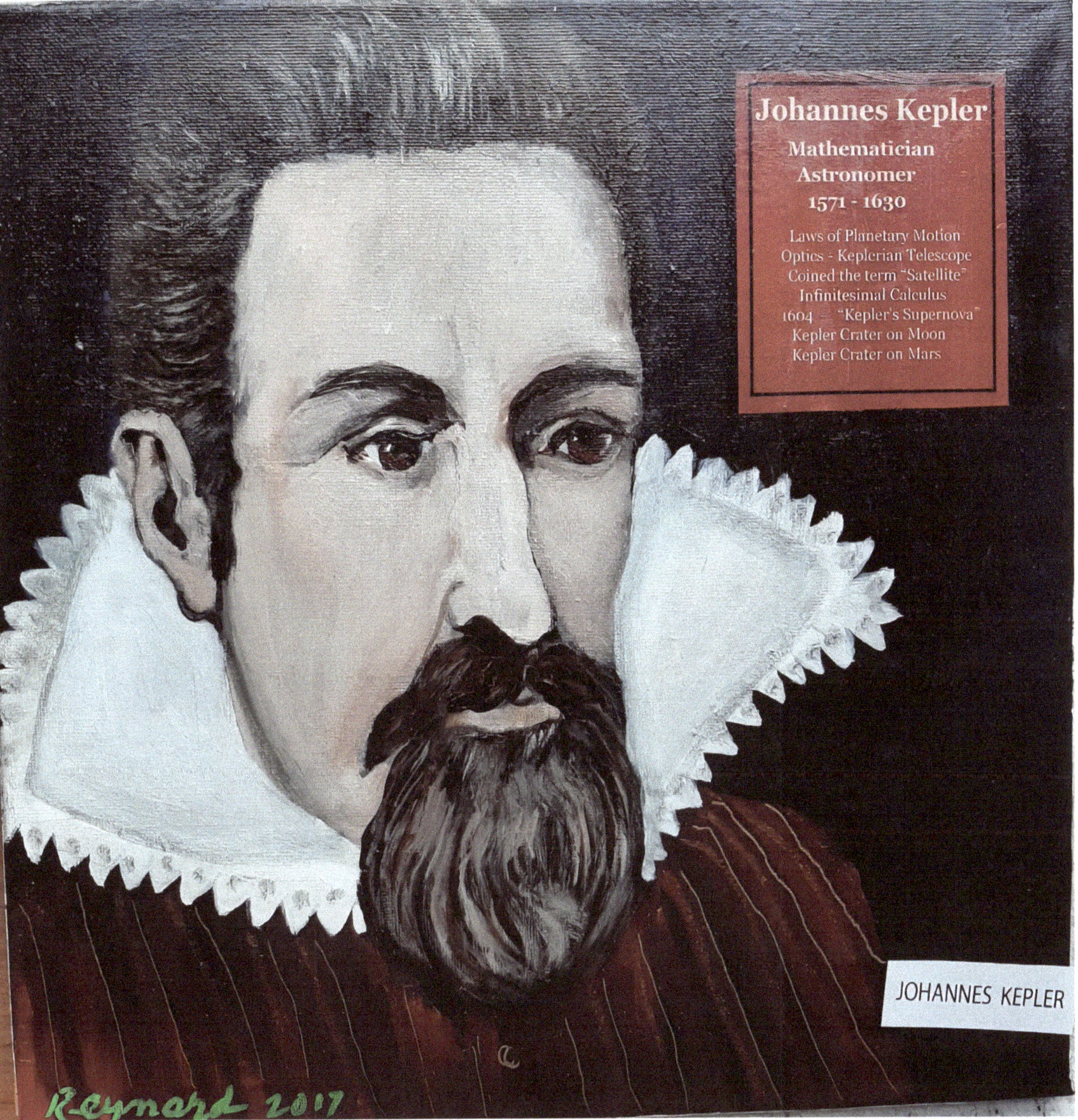

Johannes Kepler
Mathematician
Astronomer
1571 - 1630

Laws of Planetary Motion
Optics - Keplerian Telescope
Coined the term "Satellite"
Infinitesimal Calculus
1604 — "Kepler's Supernova"
Kepler Crater on Moon
Kepler Crater on Mars

JOHANNES KEPLER

Reynard 2017

Maria Mitchell:
Guiding the Stars through Uncharted Skies
1818–1889

Maria Mitchell was born in 1818, on an island called Nantucket in Massachusetts. When she was a child, her dad taught her how to use a telescope and showed her the wonders of the night sky. She loved it so much that she decided she wanted to be an astronomer, which is a scientist who studies stars, planets, and other things in space. She may have read about Kepler's discoveries as she learned about the objects in space.

One night, when she was just twenty-nine years old, Maria did something incredible: she discovered a new comet! A comet is like a giant snowball flying through space, and finding one is a huge deal. Because of this discovery, she became very famous and even got a gold medal from the king of Denmark!

Maria Mitchell was the first American woman to become a professional astronomer. She loved teaching others about the stars, so she became a professor and taught students at Vassar College in Poughkeepsie, New York. She inspired many young people, especially girls, to be curious about science and to follow their dreams.

Maria was a founder of the Association for the Advancement of Women, the first woman member of the American Academy of Arts and Sciences, and one of the first women members of the American Philosophical Society. She was also one of the first women to work for the US federal government.

Maria believed that everyone should have the chance to learn and explore, no matter who they are. She worked hard to make sure that girls had the same opportunities as boys to study and become scientists. She taught us to always look up at the stars, study, dream big, and never stop exploring!

Maria Mitchell became the first professional female astronomer in the United States. How does her determination inspire you to pursue your interests?

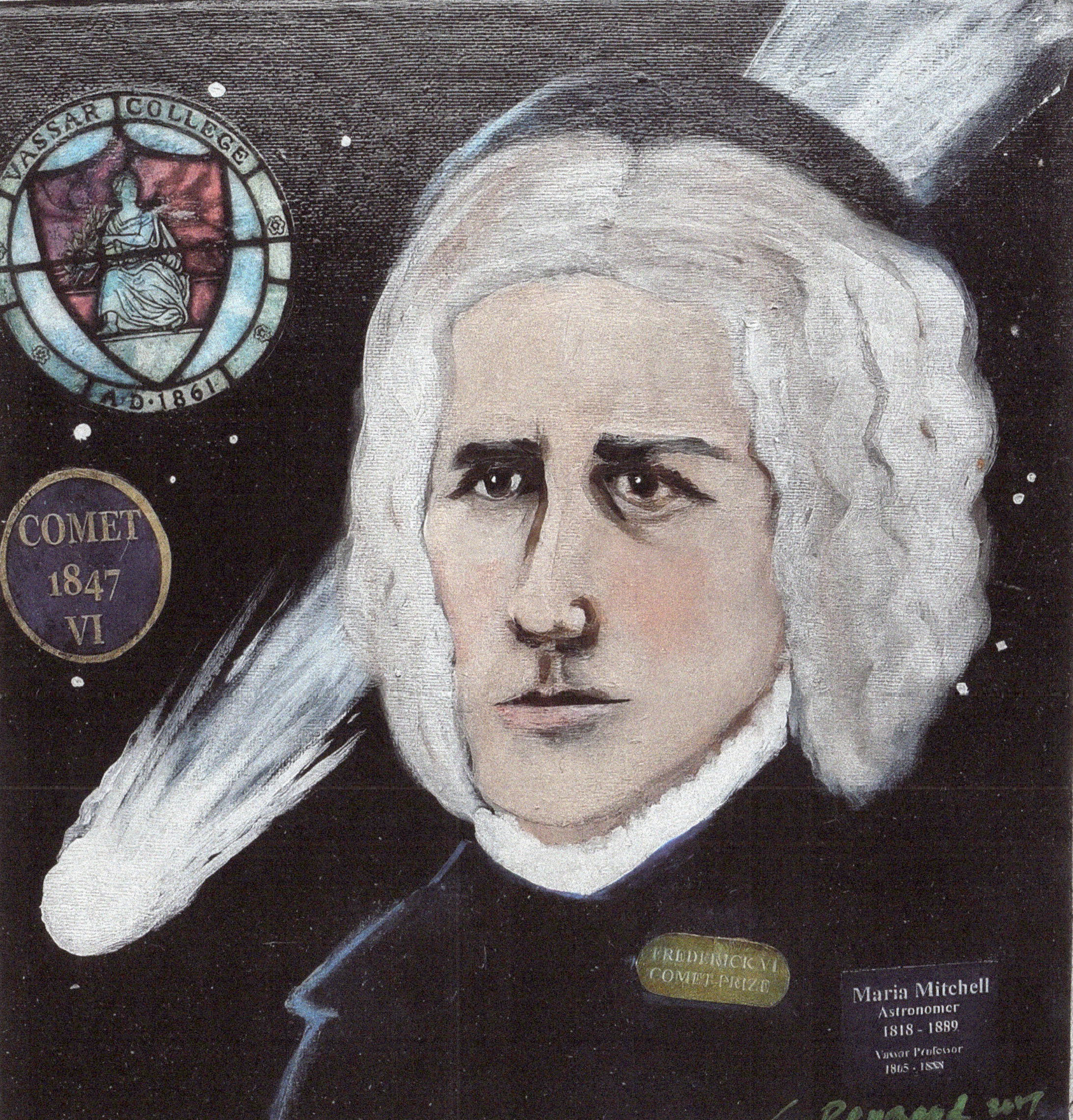

VASSAR COLLEGE
A.D. 1861
COMET
1847
VI
FREDERICK VI
COMET-PRIZE
Maria Mitchell
Astronomer
1818 - 1889
Vassar Professor
1865 - 1889

ARTHUR EDDINGTON:
JOURNEY TO THE EDGE OF THE UNIVERSE
1882–1944

Arthur Eddington was a scientist who loved studying the stars and the universe. He was born in 1882 in England. As a child, he was really curious about how things worked in space.

When Arthur grew up, he became a famous astronomer and physicist. One of his biggest discoveries was during a solar eclipse in 1919. He showed that starlight bends when it passes close to the sun. Albert Einstein had predicted this with his theory of relativity, but it was Arthur's discovery that supported Einstein's theory. This was a huge deal because it proved Einstein was right and changed how we understand gravity and the universe!

Even though Arthur Eddington didn't win a Nobel Prize himself, his work helped prove Einstein's ideas, and Einstein won the Nobel Prize later because of it.

Arthur Eddington spent his life exploring the mysteries of space and teaching others about the wonders of the universe. What's something mysterious in space that you'd like to learn more about?

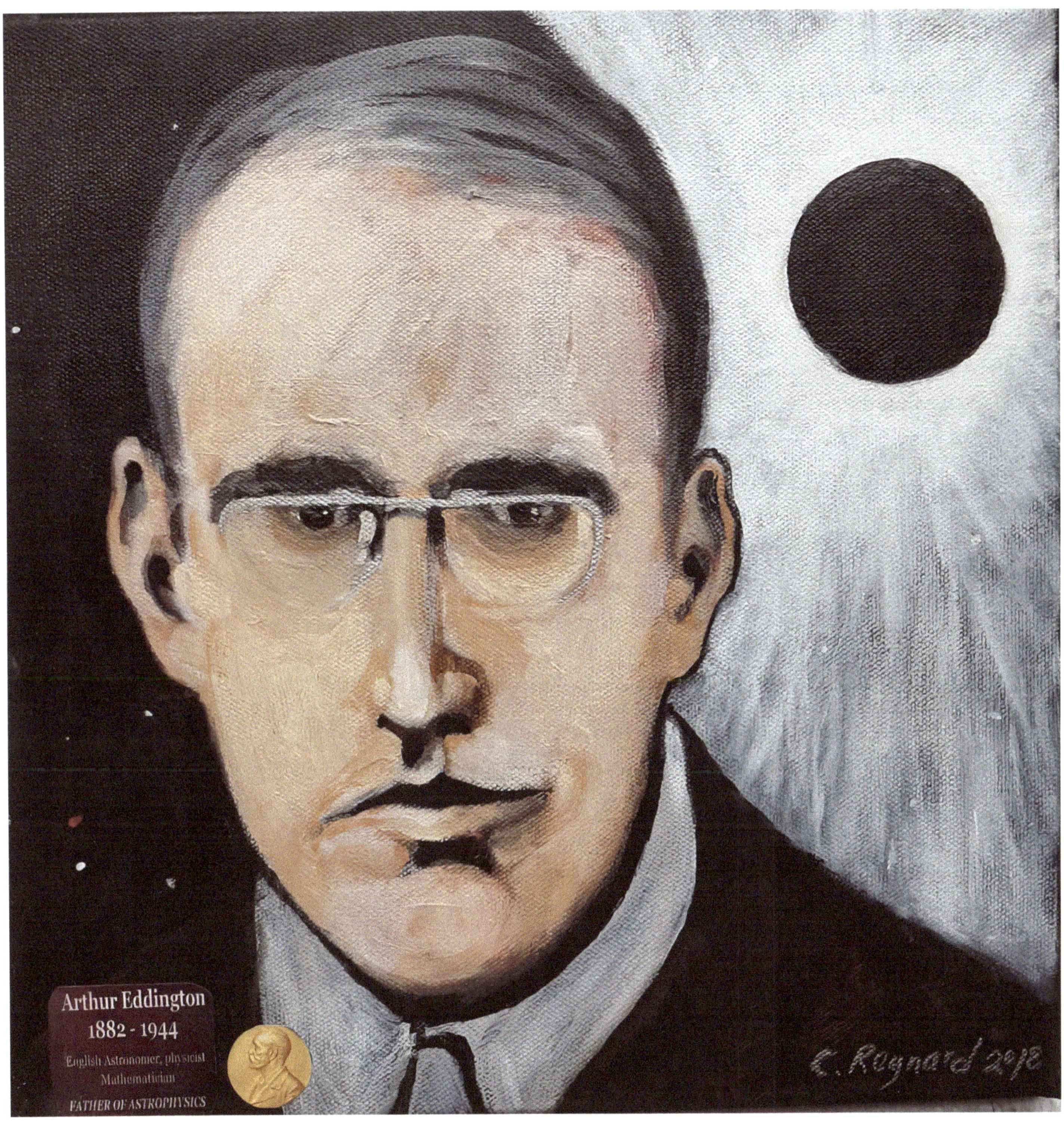

Arthur Eddington
1882 - 1944
English Astronomer, physicist
Mathematician
FATHER OF ASTROPHYSICS
C. Reynard 2018

GEORGE GAMOW:
PIONEERING THE COSMIC FRONTIER
1904–1968

George Gamow was a fun-loving scientist who was born in the city of Odesa, Russia, which is now part of Ukraine. He loved to play with ideas and imagine how the universe works. He was really interested in how atoms work and how the universe began. He came up with an idea called the big bang theory. This theory says that the universe started as a tiny, super-hot, and dense point, and then it exploded and started expanding, creating everything we see around us.

Even though the idea sounds big and serious, George had a playful way of explaining it. He wrote a book called *Mr. Tompkins in Paperback*, where he tells funny stories about a character named Mr. Tompkins, who travels through space and time and learns about the universe in silly and exciting ways.

George was also a great teacher who loved sharing his excitement about science with others. He explained complicated ideas in simple and funny ways so everyone could understand.

Even though George Gamow passed away in the late 1960s, his playful spirit and love for science still inspire us today. He showed us that learning about the universe can be fun and exciting, just like solving a big puzzle or going on a fantastic adventure!

George Gamow was a cosmic comedian, using his imagination and humor to explore the mysteries of the universe and share the joy of discovery with everyone around him! Just like George Gamow loved to tell stories about space and atoms, what's a funny way you could explain a scientific idea you've learned to a friend?

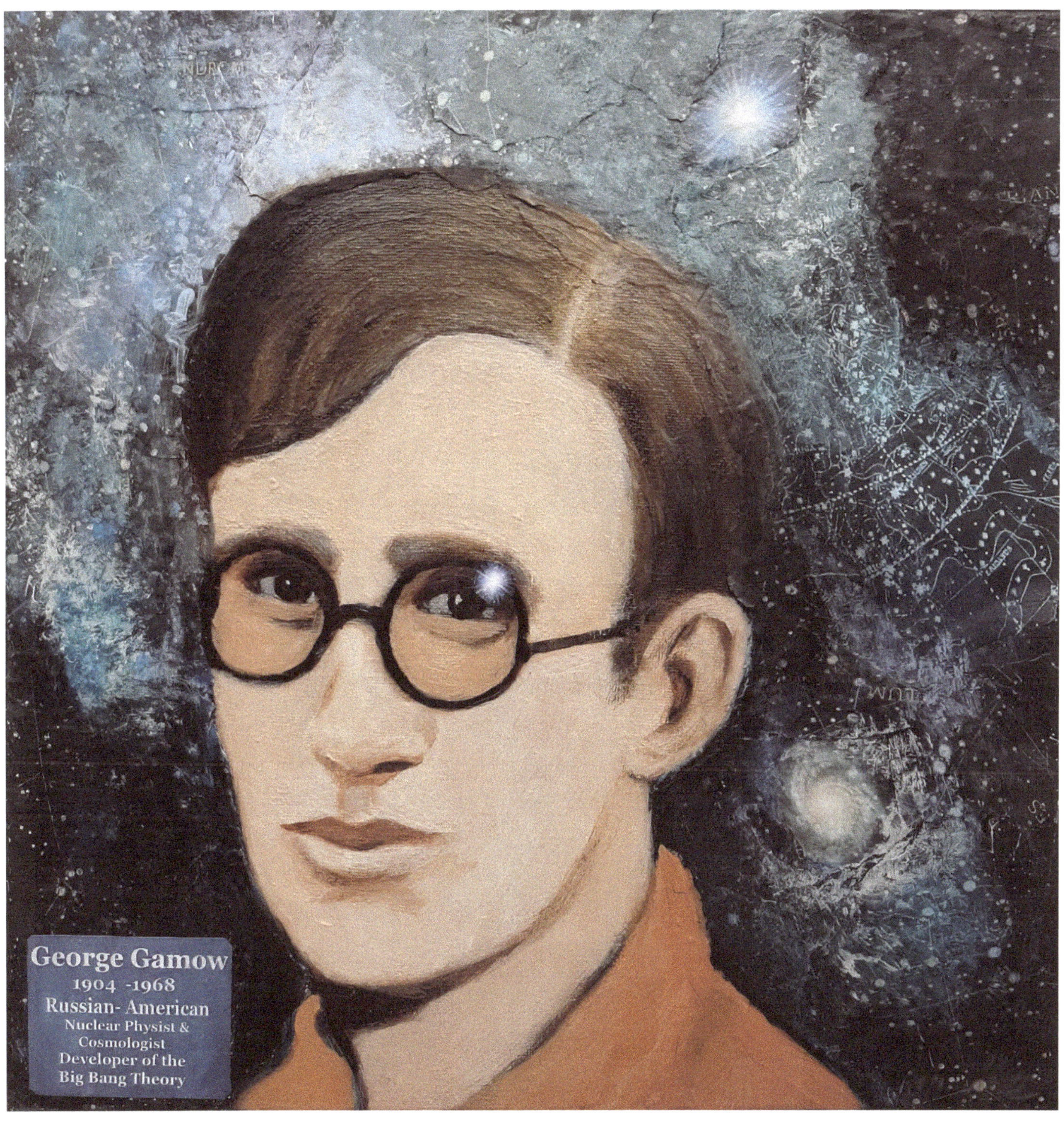

George Gamow
1904 -1968
Russian- American
Nuclear Physist &
Cosmologist
Developer of the
Big Bang Theory

EDWIN HUBBLE:
BEYOND THE MILKY WAY
1920–2006

Edwin Hubble was an amazing astronomer who was born in Marshfield, Missouri. He loved exploring the vastness of space and discovering the secrets of the universe. He used powerful telescopes to observe faraway galaxies and stars.

One of Hubble's biggest discoveries was that the universe is expanding. This means that everything in the universe is moving away from each other, like raisins in a rising loaf of bread.

He also discovered that there are other galaxies beyond our own Milky Way. Before his work, people thought that our galaxy was the only one in the universe. Hubble showed that there are billions of other galaxies out there, each with its own stars, planets, and mysteries.

Hubble's discoveries helped us understand how the universe is changing and evolving. He even has a super cool space telescope named after him, called the Hubble Space Telescope, which takes amazing pictures of distant galaxies and helps scientists today learn even more about the universe.

Edwin Hubble was an explorer of the cosmos, using his telescope to uncover the wonders of space and inspiring us all to look up at the stars and dream of the endless possibilities of the universe!

Like Edwin Hubble, who discovered that the universe is expanding, have you ever made an unexpected discovery while observing something in nature or space?

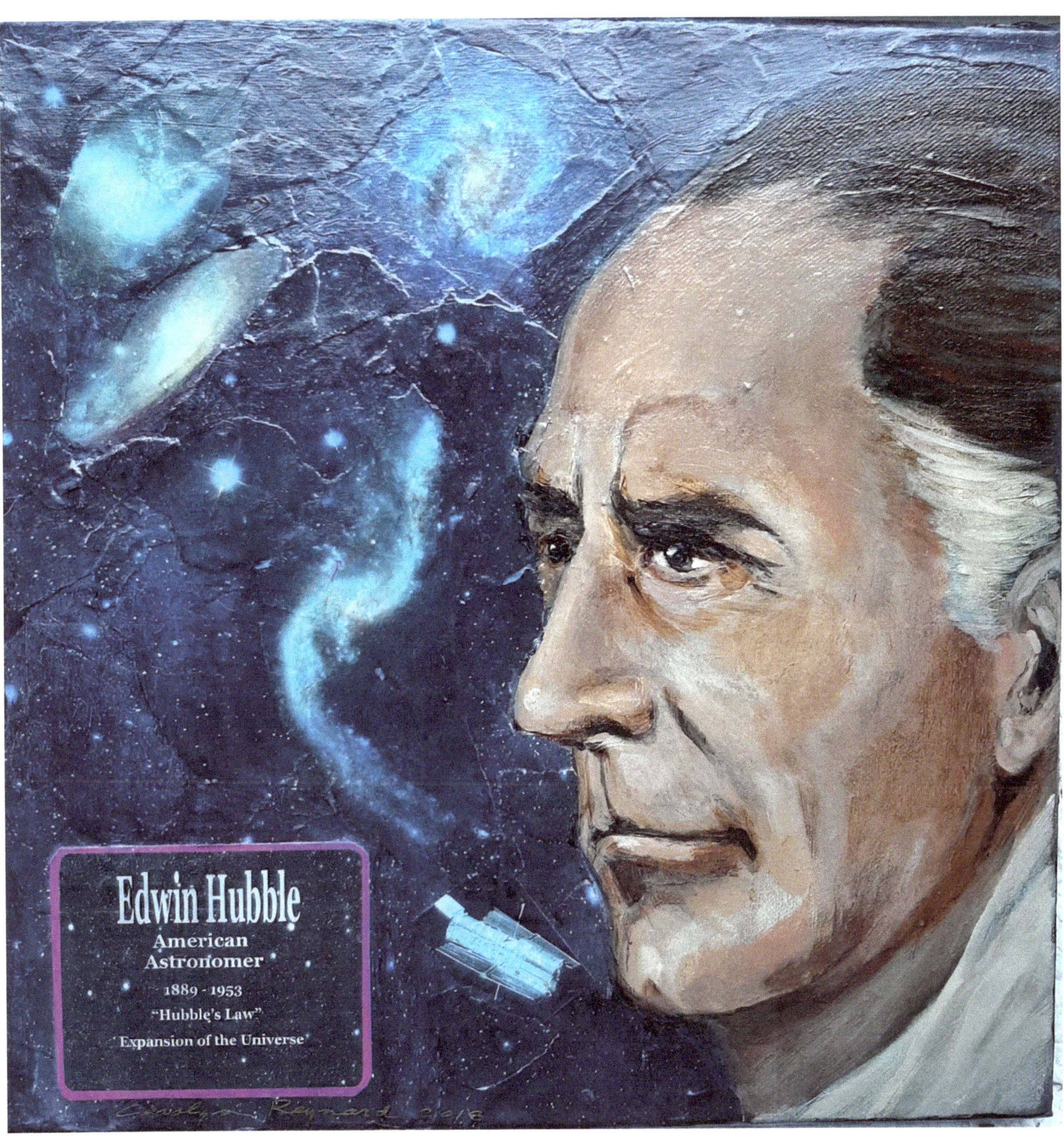
Edwin Hubble
American Astronomer
1889 - 1953
"Hubble's Law"
Expansion of the Universe

STEPHEN HAWKING: STARGAZER'S TRIUMPH
1942–2018

Stephen Hawking was a brilliant man who loved thinking about the biggest and most mysterious things in the universe. Imagine someone who looks up at the stars and wonders about black holes, time travel, and how the universe began. That was Stephen!

When Stephen Hawking was a young boy, growing up in Oxford, England, he was already very interested in astronomy, the study of objects outside Earth's atmosphere, such as the sun, moon, planets, stars, and galaxies. He built a telescope with his friends and spent many nights exploring the cosmos from his backyard in England. This early fascination with astronomy and his study of other astronomers and their theories planted the seeds for his future groundbreaking discoveries about the universe.

Stephen developed a disease when he was twenty-one years old that made it hard for him to move and talk, but he didn't let that stop him! He used a special computer to help him speak and share his amazing ideas.

Stephen was very curious about black holes. These are places in space where gravity is so strong that nothing, not even light, can escape. He discovered that black holes aren't completely black. Instead, they can give off tiny bits of energy, which we now call Hawking radiation. This was a really big discovery!

He also wrote a famous book called *A Brief History of Time*, where he explained his ideas about the universe in a way that everyone could understand. People all over the world read his book and got excited about space and science.

Stephen Hawking showed us that even if you have big challenges, you can still achieve amazing things with curiosity and determination. He inspired many people to look at the stars and wonder about the incredible mysteries of our universe.

Stephen Hawking explored the mysteries of black holes and the universe using his brilliant mind and a computer. How do you use technology to explore and learn about the world?

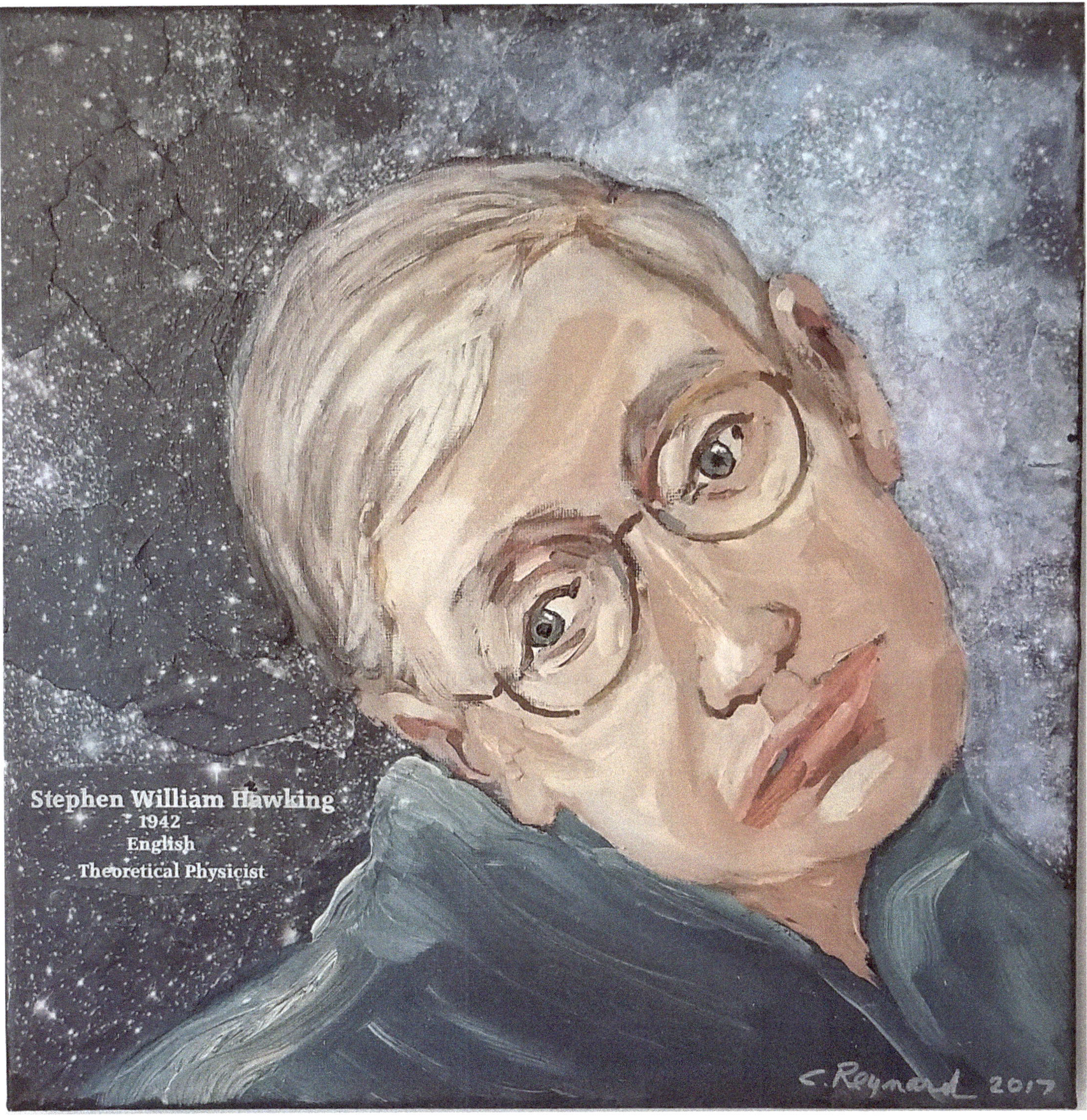
Stephen William Hawking
1942 –
English
Theoretical Physicist
C. Reynard 2017

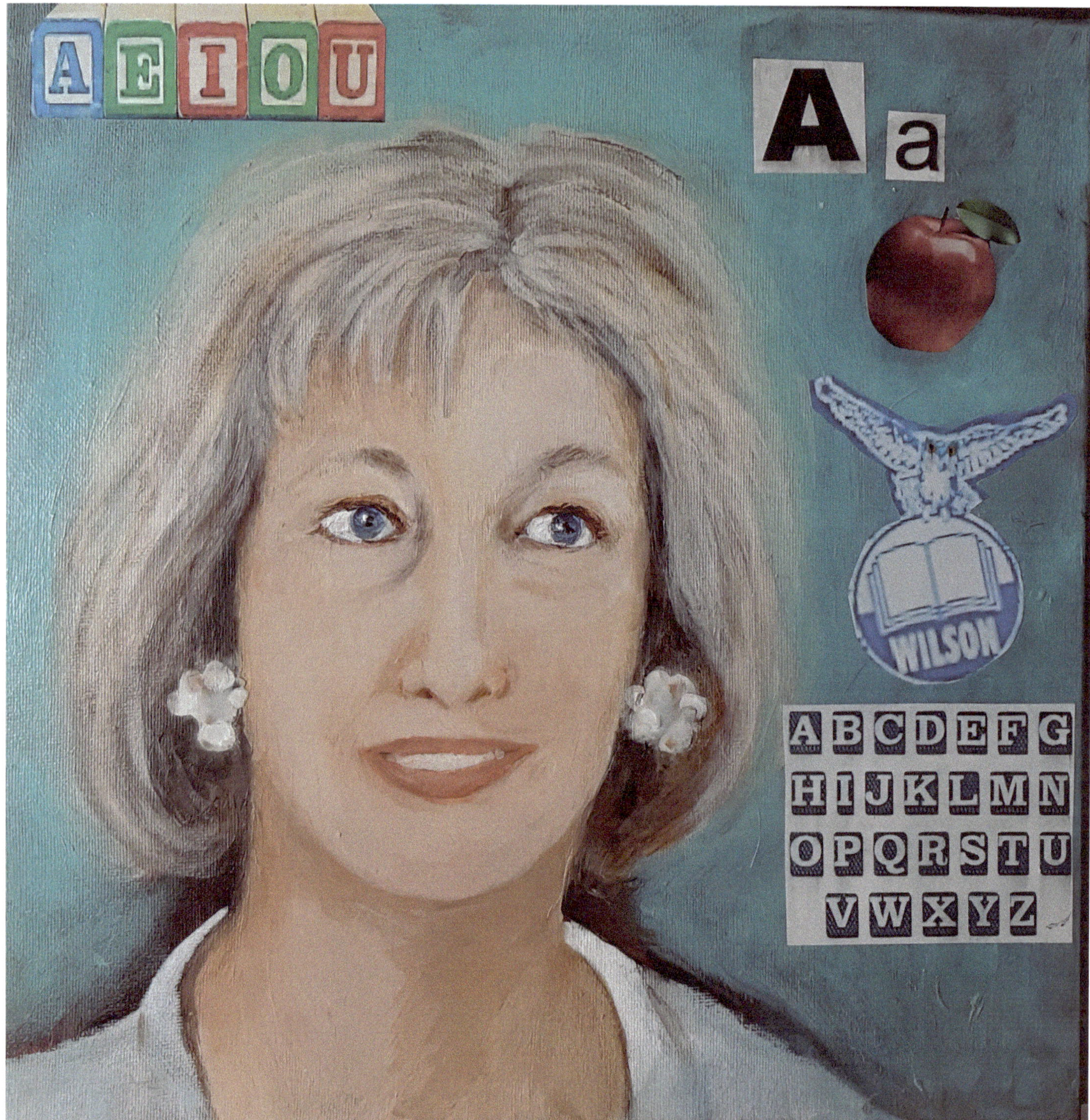

A E I O U
A a
WILSON
ABCDEFG
HIJKLMN
OPQRSTU
VWXYZ

ABOUT THE AUTHOR, TERESA (TERRY) BRUSCO

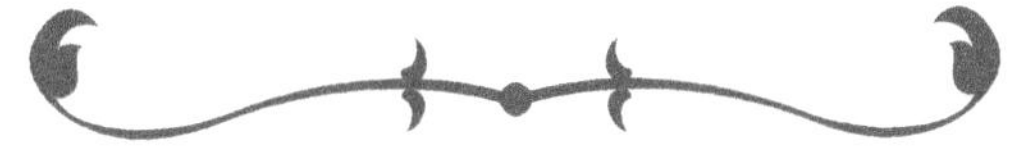

As a native of Vermont, Teresa Brusco's childhood was deeply rooted in the woods, where she nurtured a curiosity for the natural world. Upon attending college in New Haven, Connecticut, her academic focus centered on education and psychology. This led her to embark on a career as a special education teacher in Wappinger Falls, New York, dedicated to empowering elementary-aged students facing learning challenges. This is where she met her dear friend, colleague, and artist, Carolyn Reynard.

Over the span of thirty-five years in the classroom, Teresa honed her expertise in reading instruction, specializing particularly in supporting dyslexic students for an additional six years before retiring from public school in 2013. Subsequently, she spent a decade at Wilson Language Training (WLT), where she provided extensive support and collaborative coaching to educators across the United States involved in learning the WLT structured literacy programs.

Teresa's journey has been defined by a passion for teaching and a commitment to enhancing educational outcomes for all students, particularly those with unique learning needs.

ART, ROCKS, BRUSHES, AND KINDNESS:
THE ARTISTIC JOURNEY OF CAROLYN REYNARD
1934–2023

Carolyn Reynard was an incredible woman who loved both art and science and spent her life sharing her passions with others.

Carolyn was born in Wichita, Kansas, in August 1934. She loved art from a young age and went on to study fine arts at Wichita State University and Ohio University. By the time she was twenty-four years old, she had earned a Master of Fine Arts in Painting. The very next year, she started teaching drawing and art education at Ohio University.

Carolyn later moved to California and became an art therapist at the Devereux Foundation, where she helped people feel better by using art. She then decided to move to New York, where she taught students from grades one to twelve in the Copenhagen School District and taught drawing and art education at SUNY College at Oswego.

Carolyn's adventure continued when she moved to Florida to be the coordinator and instructor of art in the DeSoto County School District. She missed the cold winters of the Northeast, so in 1969, she settled in the Hudson River Valley in New York. There, she delighted elementary school students in Wappinger Falls, NY, with her fun and inspiring art lessons.

When Carolyn retired from teaching art, she decided to follow in her father's footsteps and explore geology. Her father, Virgil Cole, was an exploration petroleum geologist, and she was inspired by his experiences to learn about rocks and the Earth. She spent time talking with both amateur and professional geologists, learning as much as she could.

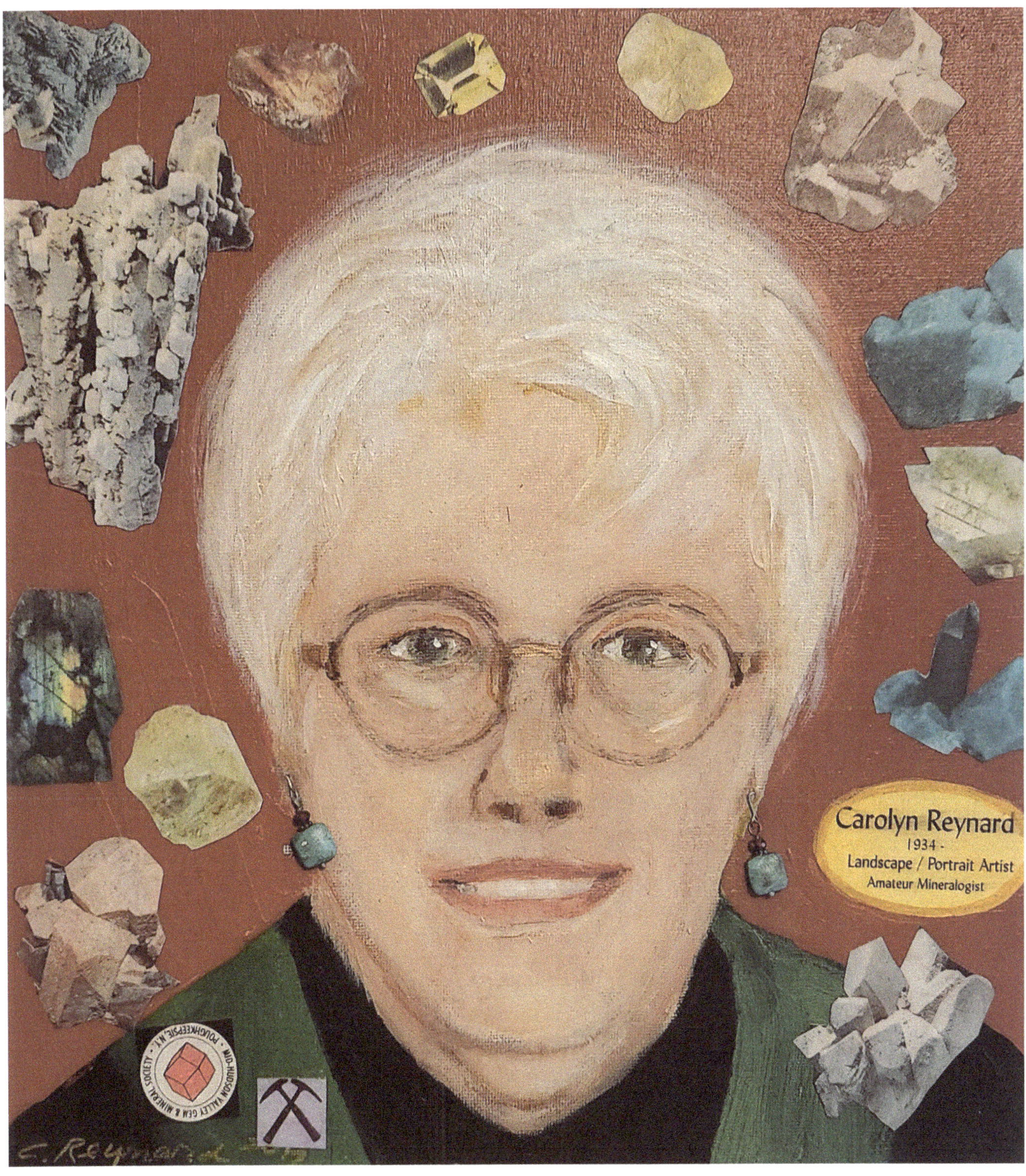

Carolyn Reynard
1934 -
Landscape / Portrait Artist
Amateur Mineralogist
POUGHKEEPSIE N.Y.
MID-HUDSON VALLEY GEM & MINERAL SOCIETY

Carolyn combined her love for art and geology in a unique way. She created beautiful artworks inspired by her scientific discoveries. She once said, "Drawing, painting, and geology have been my lifelong journey. My father provided the rock-solid foundation in science; I found my own way in the arts." Her works of art were exhibited at Vassar College in Poughkeepsie, NY, in a geology museum, showing how she brought together her two passions.

Most importantly, Carolyn's message to everyone was to be kind. She believed that kindness could make the world a better place, whether through teaching, creating art, or simply being good to others.

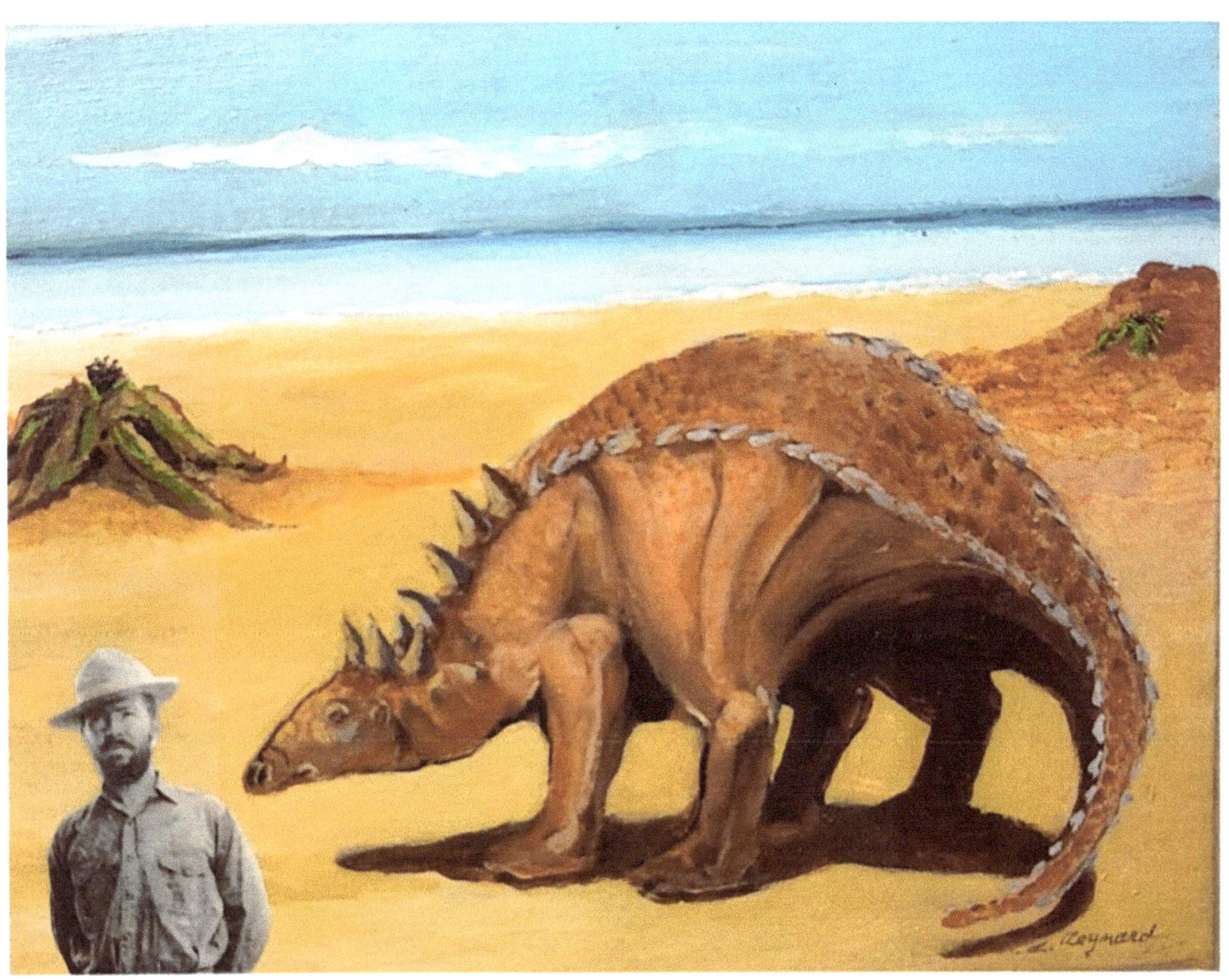